No More Procrastination: Simple Habits to Boost Your Productivity & Get Things Done

Discover How to Eliminate Procrastinating Habits & Overcome Laziness for Good

Table of Contents

INTRODUCTION 4

CHAPTER ONE: QUIT BAD HABITS NOW 8

    The Biggest Misconceptions about Laziness 8

    5 Reasons Why you are Lazy and How to Fix Them 10

    6 Ways to Overcome the Lazy Brain 14

    7 Terrible Habits that Keep you from Success 17

CHAPTER TWO: FIRING UP A MOTIVATED MIND 20

    Which Type of Procrastinator are you? 20

    10 Must-Know Hacks for Mind-Blowing Motivation 27

    The Fixed Mindset vs the Growth Mindset 31

    5 Tips for Developing a Mindset That Brings You Success 33

CHAPTER THREE: GETTING THE JOB DONE 35

    11 Essential Techniques to Power Up Your Productivity 35

    10 Secrets Behind Productivity According to the World's Billionaires 40

    5 Time Management Strategies to get More Done in Less Time 44

CHAPTER FOUR: SHARPENING FOCUS 48

    14 EXERCISES TO DEVELOP RAZOR-SHARP FOCUS 49

    The Crucial Link Between your Brain and your Belly 56

    5 Ways to Develop Unwavering Self-Discipline 58

CHAPTER FIVE: GOAL SETTING FOR SUCCESS 62

Concepts Associated with Goal Setting 63

Forms of Goals 64

10 Goal-Setting Techniques to Achieve your Goals Faster 64

7 Things you Need to Know About Setting the Right Goals 68

The Best Ways to Reward Yourself for Completed Goals........ 70

CHAPTER SIX: NEW YOU, NEW ROUTINES 74

8 Ways to Create Great Habits that Lead to Success 75

9 Morning Routine to Make Every Day a Good Day................ 81

6 Evening Routines to Ensure Tomorrow is just as Good as Today.. 85

CHAPTER SEVEN: NO MORE OBSTACLES 88

7 Ways to Conquer Your Fear of Failure 88

7 Strategies for Defeating the Monster of Perfectionism 91

7 Ways in Which Positivity can Manifest Success 94

5 Empowering Mantras to Destroy Self-Sabotage and Start Getting Stuff Done. 98

CONCLUSION... 100

INTRODUCTION

It doesn't matter what phase of your life you are currently in, or what profession you may find yourself. The truth is that all of us are all trying to overcome procrastination in one way or the other. We yearn to not only get results, but to get them fast. Results are good, but the faster they arrive, the better for us. And this is where procrastination comes in.

Most of us already have everything planned out. Our heads a bubbling with a lot of ideas and visions, and we want to get started as soon as possible, but procrastination holds us back from achievement. It is so subtle that you never know that you are being held back.

Most people who procrastinate actually end up completing their tasks before the deadline, but they mostly face the pressure of completing a job under pressure. A procrastinator is never satisfied with the completed job even when it was completed before the deadline. There will always be this fear that something was not done right. Procrastination forces you to live in anxiety and perpetual fear.

There is hope. The first step is to understand that there is a problem. A procrastinator that doesn't know that he/she procrastinates is on the way to the largest pitfall in the world. Knowing you have a problem is the beginning of the solution. Procrastination is tricky, but it can be understood. You only have to make up your mind that you want to understand. And that is what I will be helping you do in this book: understand procrastination.

You can only break its stronghold only after understanding what makes it strong. There are little bits that can help you overcome procrastination. Do you know that the content of your stomach at any given point can have an effect on your productivity at that time? Surprising, right? But that is the case.

As you follow my guides in this book, I want to assure you that you are in safe hands. I am Ethan Grant, and I love to think as myself as a productivity agent. I am a leading speaker on the topic of productivity. I understand both the concept of productivity and procrastination, and I know how to switch them in a person.

There is something I refer to as the procrastinator psychology. It is so strong in procrastinators that they hardly ever know it exists. I will be revealing that to you during our journey through the pages of this book. I only ask that you stay with me and be as attentive and proactive to change as ever. I have designed this book in the simplest form possible so that it can benefit anyone who reads it. The steps listed are all practical ones, so you will have problems following them.

Toni Morrison noted in one of her books, "If you surrender to the air, you can ride it." There are a lot of possibilities in your life. The quantities of things you can achieve are quite overwhelming, but procrastination will never let you.

If you have ever sat down to imagine all the great things you COULD have done but didn't do, even though you are 100% sure you have all it takes, then, you should know you have a procrastination problem. But once this problem is overcome, a lot of possibilities begin to open up to you, things you had never imagined you could ever do.

The benefits of conquering procrastination are numerous. Just sit and try to imagine all of the fulfillment and purpose that could come to your life if you decide to take a step today and become productive in whatever field you may find yourself.

My productivity tips have touched lives in various places. I have people call and tell me some of the ways in which my teachings have affected their lives very positively. Over the years, I have toiled endlessly to produce some of the nuggets I will be sharing with you in this book. You should count yourself lucky because you will be receiving most of my life's work in the following chapters. These are nuggets that have changed lives and created a fresh path for people who had once been frustrated in their frustration.

Productivity is a blissful thing, but it has to be understood and respected before it can be applied. Of course, nothing good comes easy, so you will have to give the procedures in this book some time before you begin to reap the benefits. But I can assure you that if these principles are applied, there is nothing that will be able to stop your light from shining.

You might be asking, 'Why this book, out of all the other books that deal with the topic of procrastination?' The major aim of writing this book is to pour all of myself into these pages. You won't just be reading a book; you will be picking my brain and going away with wonderful knowledge.

I am a seasoned teacher, and I try to be as technical as possible with any of my written works. This is to make sure that my reader easily understands the information I am trying to pass across. If the communication gap is faulty, then, the whole writing venture is utterly pointless. It is this communication gap that I have tried to bridge in the best way possible. The method listed here are procedures that a determined person can use successfully without any stress.

Remember, Heaven only helps those who help themselves. Sitting under an apple tree does not mean you will go home with a basket full. You need to take action and plug down some for your satisfaction. Success is right there at the corner, but she will never come into your house until you ask her in. And, dear, she can be very selective, only listening to those who understand her principles.

Finally, remember that our world only belongs to action-takers. No real change can happen except you decide to take action. Action is the key ingredient in every success story. You have to begin to beat procrastination now before it snatches away your glorious destiny.

A productive lifestyle should be your major aim as you strive to become a better version of yourself. Begin to practice all the tips and guidelines provided in this book and don't falter. Results take time to come back, and it is only the steady that stand to reap the benefits of their labor. I hope you soon have a positive story to tell. Good luck as we dive in.

CHAPTER ONE: QUIT BAD HABITS NOW

The Biggest Misconceptions about Laziness

Let's start by noting that laziness is not a sickness or a personality disorder; it is mostly something you have accepted for yourself. Laziness is something that slowly creeps towards you, entangles you, and gradually takes over your personality. It is very stealthy, and it works hand-in-hand with procrastination.

Think of laziness as a desire of the layperson. It is something you want to do, something you are very comfortable with. Although a lot of people might argue and talk about how much they hate laziness, deep down inside of them, there is a part of them that is comfortable with just lying around and getting nothing done. It is almost like an inner conflict with yourself. One part of you is begging you just to achieve nothing, while the other part knows and understands the repercussions of those actions.

Take note that laziness and rest aren't the same. You rest after completing a huge project, but when this rest continues for an extended time, then you know that there is a problem. Laziness can so eat up into a personality that it becomes part of their personality, a habit that they can do nothing about. And this is where it gets weird and dangerous. At this point, the individual might begin to see laziness as a disorder or a sickness, which in most cases, is wrong.

The habit of laziness can form from a variety of circumstances. It is even more active in adults who have somehow lost motivation to be adventurous and seek out new things in the world. Study the children around you. You hardly see a lazy one. They are always up and doing, looking for the next big adventure and discovery. And that is why life stays bright and true to them because they understand the rudiments of new things.

On the contrary, laziness in an adult can result because the older person believes he has seen enough of life and is now particularly unmotivated. This is laziness of the mind. Here, the individual in question is endowed with enough strength and energy to carry out the task, but because there is no zeal, the task remains undone. And laziness is blamed.

From another perspective, laziness can be said to be a variety of states which can be emotional or physical that can affect a person's zeal to get things done. For different people, there are different reasons why they are lazy. Sometimes, laziness can spring up in a hardworking individual all because of lack of interest. Imagine an extreme introvert and extreme extrovert, both planning for parties. One will definitely put in more effort into the preparation more than the other. Now it is not that the introvert is lazy, but introverts are generally people who do not like to invest in social activities.

But this shouldn't be an excuse to accommodate laziness. A person is never born naturally lazy, except if there is a sickness that naturally weakens the individual. Apart from that, laziness is learned or walked into and becomes a habit. The funny thing about laziness as a habit is that it continues to grow on you until it completely destroys all of your plans. Laziness is one aspect of your life that can affect another part of your life and ruin it with laziness. If you get away with laziness today, your mind will try to trick you into believing you will get away with it again until the devastating finally happens.

5 Reasons Why you are Lazy and How to Fix Them

Many times, people have a bleak sense of the fact that laziness has finally crept into their life. It is no longer a question of 'Am I lazy?', but now 'Why am I lazy?' While this is a very important question, the answer to that question is not readily available except through a deeper search. There are various reasons why people end up lazy, and these reasons vary from individual to individual. Laziness can be caused by a wide range of external factors, including psychological.

A lot of revelation has been given on how to overcome laziness. Like other traits, laziness can be pulled off one's skin and replaced. Although this method works, most times the candidates applying them may drop back into laziness. But there is something quite deeper to the situation. You have to sit and understand the true cause of your own brand of laziness before a solution can be prescribed.

There are some generally identifiable causes of laziness in different individuals, no matter their personality differences. Some of these include:

1. Being overwhelmed by the task at hand.

Some people get overwhelmed by the size of the work required to complete a project. One method to get rid of this is to break down major tasks into smaller tasks, but even this itself can cause a person to ignore the task. Most times, people lack the knowledge required to go about breaking down a task. So, they just forget the task and leave it hanging. This form of laziness mostly has to do with mental capability. It is laziness that is formed because an individual cannot do the mental exercise required to understand the task at hand.

This task will require an insane amount of research, materials collection, and all other requirements. But the solution here is to learn the skills involved in breaking down a task into smaller tasks. It is not a skill that one is born with. It is developed over time, with constant practice. If you have identified this kind of laziness in your life, it is time you put effort into learning how to deal with large projects and handle it in parts, one at a time.

2. Unidentified Purpose

Unless you have established the reason why the completion of a particular task will be important to you, your mind will never put the body to the task of completing the job. When there is no clear-cut purpose, there will hardly be any motivation to complete the task. Laziness easily seems to be a safe haven for people without a clear-cut purpose to pursue.

Once a person becomes plagued with such a form of laziness, there will be no zeal to act. All that they will be looking for is a form of escape, something that will relieve them of the thought of purposelessness. If you discover that you fall into this category of laziness, the solution will be to find something that motivates you. Find something that will make you want to act. Before you start any task, sit, and list out all of the benefits you can get when the task is finally complete. This will provide you with some motivation to get the job to the next level.

3. A need to produce a perfect job

For a perfectionist, the rule is to get it done to 100% excellence or leave it undone. While this can sometimes be a very admirable trait necessary to produce the best results from a task, it can sometimes dampen a perfectionist's zeal to work. A perfectionist will spend hours and days gathering and perfecting the material requires to start up a task. The non-perfectionist, on the other hand, has already begun with what he has and has made progress. In time, he will be through with the job, putting the finishing touches to perfect the job as well as he could.

Perfectionists always get frustrated easier while working on a task because attaining perfection is never an easy task. There will always be factors on the ground that ensure that the work never attains perfection. The fear of making mistakes is another factor that holds perfectionists from starting up a task. This happens most especially when there is a portion of the job that they are not fully capable of carrying out. So, to prevent mistakes, they don't even start at all. While this might not outrightly translate into laziness, when it continues to build up, the person can begin to lose the zeal to work.

You can curb the effects of this perfectionist lifestyle by understanding that perfection is not attained in one go. It takes time to get something to be as good as you may want it to be. And that is the beauty of working on something, to put in more and more until you create something of quality. Quality takes time and effort. The joy is in the process of completing the job, and you will be fully rewarded when it is achieved. Understand that there is a time to set aside your perfectionist mindset and try to get things done, even if you are not too confident in your ability to complete the given task. Don't be scared that people will look at you differently when you fail. They, too, have failed before, so you shouldn't mind their glances. Just do what needs to be done.

4. **Accepting laziness**

There is a kind of laziness that is inhabited, laziness that you can speak yourself into. Some people have never put their minds into achieving something tangible, such that they don't even have an idea of what it is to be productive. It is more like a state of complacency and inactivity. These have a mentality that before a task can be carried out, it has to be fun and enjoyable, so whenever they are faced with a tedious task, they blank out and look for ways to escape. Things that do not fall into the enjoyable category are left for later, and then later, and finally later until they are never done.

Having these thoughts once in a while is completely normal. That is just the way your body works. But if it keeps on recurring over and over, then you know that they are a problem with your work ethic. Your body only wants to enjoy itself, which is wrong. There should be times when your body will be disciplined and made to get the job done. These thoughts can, in some ways, block your ability to produce something worthwhile, something that can be appreciated.

Strip your mind of these kinds of thoughts and get to work. See yourself as someone who has to achieve. Action taken now is always the best, and it will lead to the most satisfying rewards.

5. Health conditions

Like has been noted earlier, there is a kind of laziness that is caused by physical ailments or sickness. If you find out that you easily feel tired and there is never any motivation for you to work, then you should consider having yourself medically tested. These sicknesses hardly ever reveal themselves until it is quite late, but your body responds to them early enough, and it is left to you to detect these responses. One of such ways the body responds is to feel tired to help you conserve energy. Yet that shouldn't be the case. All of these could be as a result of a thyroid disorder. These thyroid problems could lead to diabetes, heart diseases, and other sicknesses that could weaken the body.

6 Ways to Overcome the Lazy Brain

When laziness becomes attached to a person, it can also affect their brain and make it lazy too. Your brain and your mind, most times, work hand-in-hand. And once one of them begins to accommodate the notions of laziness, the other is instantly affected. This is known as mental laziness.

Mental laziness can present itself in a variety of ways. For one thing, mental laziness can appear in the form of a disorganized and scattered mindset. Your mental faculty will always be in disarray, producing a lot of varying thoughts that mostly have no meaning. Most of these thoughts that occur as a result of the mental disarray are:

- Negative thinking.

The mind is mostly conditioned to think about the wrong things about life, always to ruminate and consider the things that have gone wrong. How do you expect to produce results when your mind is clogged with such thoughts? It will be very hard to achieve that. These negative thoughts can build up and affect you mentally, psychologically, and physically. Once your lazy brain tells your body that it is sick and it cannot perform, your body obeys and falls into laziness.

- Missing the most important things in the picture

A mind flooded with thoughts is a mind that will always be in a panic. Nothing ever stays stable. This can kind of thinking will always draw you into yourself, causing you to miss the things right in front of you.

Some of the ways in which you can control this lazy brain and bring it to book include:

1. **Guard your mind**

Be a gatekeeper for all of the thoughts that pass through your mind. Observe the thoughts as they come and go and try to figure out the pattern in which they occur. You will be able to identify the negatives and positives. Probe yourself and find out why negative thoughts have become incessant. There may be small reasons lurking around, which you may need to fix. It could be anxiety, fear of failure, or mental stress.

2. **Pay attention to each thought.**

As the thoughts come to your mind and try to produce laziness, pay attention to each and every one of them and find their root. If you are anxious about something, then find out why anxiety occurs in the first place. If you are stressed out and can't perform optimally, then try to find out how to combat this stress and restore your body to its normal functioning state. Eliminate these thoughts one by one and reduce the power of the lazy.

3. **Don't look for an escape.**

Most people are always on the lookout for things that will help them escape the present and live in a parallel universe of entertainment. While it is OK to seek some form of escape from the hustle and bustle of life, it should be checked if it becomes too much. If you find out that you are that kind of individual that relies heavily on entertainment to escape and avoid the 'disturbances' in your life, you will notice that your mind will soon begin to experience deterioration.

There are other forms of escapism that people employ to release themselves from the grip of their lives. These recreational drugs only offer you short-term pleasure and heightened consciousness. Once it wears off, you are faced with the same issue that you had been trying to escape from. Your best option if to face whatever it is head-on and conquer it once and for all.

4. Stay Mindful

Being mindful entails paying full attention to the things around you, both those that have to do with your mental state and those that have to do with the physical world around you. Don't let anything, no matter how small and infinitesimal it may be, pass you by. Enjoy life yet probe yourself and identify reasons why you enjoy certain things. While doing this, make sure to allow your mind some room for exploration. Allow your mind to wander a little, but don't allow it to travel too far lest you lose it.

5. Get Organized

Disorganization easily results in clutter, and clutter in any form is not only a distraction but a huge wet blanket. Having your personal space clogged with clutter can result in loss of motivation. A clean space always invites you to work, to get something done. A disorganized space, on the other hand, pushes you away and tells you nothing can be done.

Try to observe it for yourself. How do you feel walking into the kitchen and meeting a pile of plates waiting for you in the sink? It is natural that you would want to attend to that before putting else on fire. The mind is always more comfortable and able to organize itself to produce whenever it is presented with a clean space.

6. Seek help when necessary

There is always help for you in trying to cure your mind of laziness. All you have to is to search for it. Sometimes you might not be able to get over a distraction or temptation to stay lazy single-handedly, but with the help of others, you will find it easy to do. There will naturally be this fear to meet people for help. This might be because of an unpleasant experience in your past, but it is a necessary skill to be learned, especially when struggling with something as addictive as laziness. A little practice may be needed to acclimatize you with the basics of finding help.

7 Terrible Habits that Keep you from Success

To live a life of productivity is to become successful in whatever you may find yourself doing. And habits themselves are some of the factors that build up to produce success. It is our habits that define us that make us who we are, either as success stories or as a failure. This is why it is necessary that one builds the perfect habits to enable success. Sadly, most people have spent their lifetime building habits that foster failure and push them further away from success. Here, I will be highlighting some of those habits that could hinder your success.

1. **Inability to say 'no.'**

Sometimes you should be the bad guy and do some rejections. Not everything you are invited to participate in should be participated in. If you find it hard to say no and not feel guilty about it after, you will realize that you have stressed both your body and your soul. Also, if you keep on saying yes to everything, you will have an overwhelming schedule, which can turn out to be disastrous too.

Research has linked depression to an inability to say no because you will soon find out that you can no longer control yourself. Not saying no can derail you from your main goal and have you chasing something else simply because someone else had cajoled you into doing that.

2. **Fear of risks**

Play it smart, but don't play it safe. That is something I love to tell my students. It is natural to nurture some fear about your future, but you should never allow it to affect your work and the decisions you make. To fear risks is to ensure that you never get anything tangible. The best things will always elude you. And no matter how much you fear risks, that thing you fear will still befall you one day, so it is best to take the risk anyway. Take risks and fail and know that at least you learned something new. That is the beauty of life, to explore and discover new things.

3. **Held back by your past**

They say, "let bygones be bygones," and I couldn't agree more. Forget the thing in your past, the things of failure, and the things of success. Success, too, has a way of holding you back from achieving more. If you have achieved it before, then, you should forward and try to conquer more. Don't allow yesterday's success to prevent you from doubling your efforts and doing more. The same goes for failure too. The best thing you can do for yourself if to bury things of the past and look forward to the future.

4. **Building your life on mere talk**

This habit is deadly. It is for people who will spend most of their time talking about a vision instead of actually getting to work to make it happen. Talk is good, but the action is better. Do you know what is best? Getting to action immediately. Don't allow the sweet stories in your mouth clog up your mind until you begin to ignore the main work that has to be done. Talk is cheap, and action is expensive. Don't live a cheap life. It is dangerous.

5. **Playing blame games**

Blame is a heavy burden, and it is a beautiful thing to get it off your shoulders. You instantly experience freedom, and you can go back to relaxing. It stays sweet until it becomes too late when you finally discover what the damage of throwing blames has cost you. If you are to be blamed, there is no need to reject the blame for the sake of temporary freedom. Accept your blame and move forward with it. Instead of making excuses and trying to free yourself, try finding out why that venture failed in the first place. Throwing blame around is a recipe for more failure.

6. **Lack of self-discipline**

   Self-discipline is simply obeying yourself as your own boss. Self-discipline is stooping low so that you are humble enough to listen to your own self. You should be able to talk yourself towards success and out of failure. In fact, you can never succeed if you have not learned how to scold yourself when necessary. Apart from that, you should fear the deadlines you place. There should be punishments for not completing a task at the right time. These are some of the things that self-discipline entails. In the end, it is all about being your own toughest master and teacher.

7. **A competitive mindset**

Subscribing to healthy competition is suitable for your development, but when competition begins to lead to envy and low self-esteem, it becomes dangerous. Your major completion should be yourself. Improve yourself irrespective of the success of others or what they are embarking on at the moment. Allow other people's success to become a motivation to drive to work, not to drive you insane. Stay in your lane, but ensure that you make that lane the best it can be.

CHAPTER TWO: FIRING UP A MOTIVATED MIND

You might be surprised that, while things might get tough, only now, you lose the drive to continue because it is just about you. Of course, the only "being" you see around is your inner self. And even your inner will to push forward has been stricken with a deadly disease I call frustration.

Do not fret! You eventually get to that stage. In fact, it is a big sign that you are progressing. It shows that you have scaled through the starter's level. Although the progress might appear slow and it might not mean much compared to the goal you have set to achieve, you are now in a position where you need to get motivated.

Be careful not to express this feeling of frustration into your daily life. The consequential effect is that nothing will seem to work for you. Why? Because you have preconditioned it as a reality to live with.

Two things might set in, discouragement and procrastination. Discouragement because you are not sure if it's going to work. And procrastination because your progress is slow. Neither of these is a deal to settle for, and other harmful things might follow.

This chapter will explore all you need to know on how to keep going.

Which Type of Procrastinator are you?

It will be interesting to note the importance of productivity at our workplace and in our daily lives. But one thing that destroys our creative ability to do more is procrastination. Procrastination is simply the act of pushing the accomplishment of things to the future; things you consider of less value in your present moment.

We all have been in this pool before. Admitting this fact doesn't present it as a good habit to do. Although prioritizing might redefine the content of the tasks pushed to the future, it only shows that we have been able to identify the root of age-old difficulties. Some might tend to shift responsibility to another time because they feel that they are incapable of doing such a task. Others might just be to fulfill another act of laziness.

1. The Evader

There are times when we are at our best to accomplish a task. But sometimes, we just decide not to continue because we worry that we can't do it. Self-doubt then kills creativity in us. You are scared that you might flop, and the only thing that comes to your mind is to push it forward. No one will argue the fact that it is good to recognize our limitations and weakness. It is also necessary that you don't allow it to hold you back.

Build a sense of importance

Understand the value attached to the task you avoid. See those values as commitments that need life support. Of course, you are the one who secures its existence by accomplishing it. And since life support is not a decision to avoid, your tasks shouldn't also. You may tend to compare each of those jobs you push further as your heartbeat. As much as our heartbeat is essential in the future, it is considered as of greater importance for the present also.

Breaking out of the evader

- Outline a positive outcome

Create enough reasons not to avoid the task. The joy of achievement alone should be a constant motivation to spark you up. While you have been a continuous benefactor of the satisfaction and pleasure derived from not doing it immediately, you can also get that fulfillment when you think of it positively.

- Gear up your will

Everything inside you must receive the right knowledge to do things quickly. And the good thing about willpower is that you are the best influencer.

- Start in pieces

Work can be overwhelming sometimes; but with strategy, it will become interesting. Break down the process of completing the task into parts. Don't think of achieving it in a stretch. Allot each piece with a time limit, say for 5 minutes (you are in control here). You might need to declutter your bedroom. Give three minutes to arrange your sneakers and two minutes to sort out a tie. Going with this flow makes the job quite more manageable and exciting.

2. The Stickler

Excellence is a virtue that should be seen in everyone; but it shouldn't affect the completeness of a job. Some people are stuck in the circle of bringing out the best in everything they do. They can't do less until they are satisfied that the work is world-class.

No one is negating the just essentials of doing things in the best way; it proves the importance of productivity. But understand that in many cases, the attention required for such tasks needs to be well monitored; and so, we tend to push it forward because we are overwhelmed. There is this fear of low standard that denies them to start off immediately.

Breaking out of the stickler
- Do the analysis

Mathematics wouldn't be necessary here, but you can think of doing the arithmetic of the last job you did. Ask yourself different questions ranging from when you started to how did you complete it. Was there any consequential effect attached to it? Were you able to attain a 100% success rate? Was there any reward of internal satisfaction to this? What outlook did it give your job? It is more likely that you have been too hard on yourself to perfect your next task, and that's why you want to fix the slightest details.

- Have a clear intent

Understand the nature of the work to be done. The technicalities, modules of operation, design outlay, and presentation. Be sure to have a clear definition of what you need to achieve. When your purpose is clear, you will not be distracted.

- Define your satisfaction

A functional analysis would make this step easier for you. Once you have been able to itemize what your happiness is, looking for it in every job you do would not be a problem again. Your satisfaction might come when you achieve, say, the right mix of color in your interior designs.

3. The Cluttered Brain

Yes, clutter! It might be true that we are really busy with many things to do. Ranging from work to social group activities, religious commitment, health and safety checks, family upkeep, and so many more engaging routines. Multiple office tasks alone at your workplace might be a threat to prioritize your daily job. It then becomes a problem to choose the right task to do at the moment. And when this gets too much for us, we tend to do some tasks and push others to the future. Sometimes, our mental state is as busy as our workload that we get confused from within first, then the reality of the physical adds insult to injury. It is apparent that you are occupied with many things to do, and the slightest time to rest is also used to think. You would agree with me that those thoughts aren't as productive as they should.

Breaking out of the cluttered brain

- Set priorities

Identify the most relevant job at hand and do them immediately. Don't ever get overwhelmed when minor tasks seem to be the large chunk of the situation. Create an express list of your routine tasks. Do the ones you feel is both necessary and urgent right away, and steadily complete others.

- Determine a deadline

As much as the job is essential, it is vital to set a time limit for each of your task. Taking too much time on a particular problem leaves others piling. Note that your time limit must be achievable. Since most of your works are routinely done, devise a strategy to simplify the process.

- Work with facts

Seek the counsel of the experts on specific tasks. Taking a step like this gives you an edge to succeed at a faster rate. Work with proven facts and figures from professionals and ease your workload burden.

- Delegate responsibilities

You don't have to necessarily do all the work. Seek the help of a colleague or, better still, allow your office assistant to do a part of the job. Be careful, though, in delegating power. Ensure that you take the critical decisions and monitor the progress of any delegated duties.

4. Carefree

These people do not see any reason to do a particular task at its proposed time. They feel that there is enough time to do the job. Fun is being derived from this act, and nothing seems to make more sense than taking hands-off work.

Remember when you needed to write a college report for a field trip, and the experience from this exercise encouraged you to plan for the next one? What happened is that you spent a lot of time fantasizing about the next trip but not into writing the report. So, the time meant for the critical task of getting the description ready was used for something else which might not be as important presently.

A fraction of this group believes that they are most effective when the deadline is close. So, they feel pressured to put in their best at the very last hour.

Breaking out of the carefree
- Do statistics for arithmetic

You might not be familiar with this principle. It's simple. Since you really don't see a reason to do the most crucial task at the moment, try applying the same principle to what you would have done at that moment. Try procrastinating your fun-filled activities. Experimenting on this will give you another sense of urgency to undertake tasks.

- Count the effects

You might need to be truthful to yourself here: What you really want is fun. But how much has this fun cost you? Think of a greater sense of accomplishment you would have had if you don't push the task to the future. There is no harm in attempting something good, so give it a try.

- Examine your triggers

You might not be aware that the source of your procrastination is not really you, but what you do at some point. Your environment might be a trigger. Do a brief examination of the things you do and see if you can do them in another way. Apply the same principle for your tasks too. It might interest you to discover what pushes you to procrastinate.

5. The fantasizer

If you belong to this group, it means you have spent a lot of time having plans but didn't take any constructive step to accomplish it. It looks quite easy to talk about reading five chapters of a book per day. In fact, you might have initiated this whole idea to your colleagues, but the stage of presenting it was the last effort made to achieve it. Understand that a proposed action without a constructive strategy remains a fantasy.

Breaking out of the fantasizer

- Understand goal setting

Starting with a plan is not a wrong move, just that the approach to achieve it must be accurately spelled out. Goal setting takes a commitment of not giving up even in the face of distractions. You will need to take every suggestion given in Chapter Five of this book seriously.

- Start small

There is no need to rush to get to the height you have always imagined. Take your time to do your task. Remember what you want to achieve will not come automatically.

- Get real

Stop wasting time on what is not achievable. If what you have always planned to do is unrealistic, its time to cut them short and get real.

10 Must-Know Hacks for Mind-Blowing Motivation

Excellence is a thing to think of when aiming at achieving goals. Lots of factors would need attention to actualize this, and one of them is motivation. Motivation is that force that keeps you going in the face of challenges and distractions. To meet your targets, you would need to keep moving to enhance your productivity level and boost your performance.

1. **Begin Little**

   One big killer of achievement is when you don't see yourself doing more, especially the way you have fantasized it. It wouldn't come as you thought. Understand that what should matter most to you whenever you are starting something new is progress.

   It might look tiresome because you feel you are not moving at the same pace as others'. That might be another mistake also. This is you doing your own thing, so you don't have any obligation to work at anyone's speed. Checking other people's progress should inspire you to do more, not to enslave you into regret.

   The reality of a long-term goal is that it requires a long period to be achieved. So take it slow and steady until you finally meet your targets. You don't need to fret.

2. **Identify a Strong Purpose**

   You shouldn't undertake anything when you have not outlined the intent. It is necessary because this will serve as a reminder any time you want to give up. Your purpose should be firm and essential to you. This assurance is what upholds your willpower.

Your intent might stem from your childhood experience, goal setting, career choice, family background, and so on. Whatever it is, it must be convincing to you. Be careful not to be enticed by the environmental factors. Don't take a course of action because that is the trend in your immediate environment. Be sure that you have thought about it very well and you are ready to go through it.

3. **Design a Structure for your Goals**

You need to differentiate yourself from everyone else. Remember that your intentions have a deadline, so nothing should distract you from fulfilling it. Create a guide that will help you focus. It can be an express outline of your targets or a picture containing what you want to achieve. Doing this brings clarity of purpose. You then know every input/resource needed to achieve success.

With a structure, you will be able to track your progress at every point in time. If it is necessary to report to anyone, your composition would have mapped it out. You wouldn't get tired of achieving an outstanding result because your progress is evident. Having a well-defined structure makes you advance in the essential details. It is a sure model for motivation.

4. **Add Fun to your Task**

No one is encouraged to do more when everything seems tedious, especially when it is a routine task. Position your job as part of your life that deserves happiness. And an excellent way to stay happy while doing your work is when you add fun to it. You don't have to be rigid here, and your job might not necessarily be a treat.

Also, don't forget that discipline should not be a lamb to sacrifice for pleasure. Play your favorite playlist while you type and enjoy the rhythm. You may also decide to chat with your colleague during your break. Speak lavishly about what makes the job interesting.

5. **Look Out for your Tribe**

Tribe here means people of the same kind. It might be a colleague that has decided to be on the same course of action with you. You might have decided to write a review for five international magazines on a particular theme. Check someone around you who have made the same decision too.

You will get more inspired because you are sure that you are not alone on this journey of success. Seeing the other person(s) creates a mindset of competition. Make it more fun when you meet with them by challenging your abilities. Your aim here is not to feel awkward even if you don't meet the target given to you. The teamwork spirit should get you going.

6. **Avoid Negative Thoughts**

Naturally, diverse ideas will flow through your mind, whether you are doing well or not. But you can sieve whatever comes to your mind. Be in control of what dominates your thoughts, especially negative ones. A better way to maintain good ideas is to have positive affirmations whenever a bad one flashes in your mind. You might be thinking of not achieving the task because you feel you are incapable. Tell yourself that "I am not deficient of abilities, and I will have productive and outstanding results."

7. **Learn more**

Task yourself to learn about a particular task. The good thing about knowledge is that it set you further beyond expectation. Many people have actually gone through what you are thinking of doing. Read about them. Learn the different challenges they faced and how they overcome them. Reading their stories will position you to have extensive experience as you won't need to fall victim to the circumstances. Read newspapers, magazines, and blogs; watch videos, and get yourself inspired by your discoveries.

8. **See a Professional**

Their job is to guide you through extraordinary sessions. Your aim here is not to limit yourself to what you hear. An encounter with the experts makes the job more personal. You will be able to relate your fears, frustrations, and challenges with an open mind. At the end of the day, you must have been held accountable for the procedural counsel. You could also sharpen your leadership skills with a professional. And if the success of what you want is a priority, don't think about the cost attached to seeking the help of a professional.

9. **Step Back Frequently**

Working smart is the key to a successful work outcome. You don't have to get stuck over a task for too long just because you want to find a solution. Restore your mental capabilities by taking breaks. Your health is most valuable when you need to get going. You would agree that you are less productive whenever you spend more time than necessary. You might be trying to design a book cover, but it seems the dots are not connecting. Leave the job for a while. Take a walk down the street or probably surf the internet. During that break period, your brain and other parts of your body would have been refreshed, leaving you better than before.

10. Live Healthily

No one can take care of you better than you. Look out for nutrient-giving foods. You might consider eating vegetables and fruits, depending on your diet. Taking water frequently is quite healthy. The focus here is that your physical body must be able to sustain every activity you intend to do. Living in sickness is enough discouragement to perform any task.

The Fixed Mindset vs the Growth Mindset

The subject of mindset is important because what we make of it determines our productivity level and success rate. Mindset is the collection of ideas (stemming from personal to environmental, cultural, and spiritual experience), assumptions, beliefs, and thoughts held up to become a constituent part of inclination, interpretations, disposition, and mental habit. It is then crucial to master the art of mindset both for personal or professional use. The effect of mindset is shown at the behavioral level and creates a rigid perspective about life in general.

The Fixed Mindset

As the name implies, a fixed mindset holds that their daily-life attributes are static traits, and therefore cannot be modified. People with this mindset focus more on what they can do as fuelled by their intelligence, ability, and talents. Any effort that leads to success is not an option to them. They somewhat vouch on their talent alone instead of adopting strategies to improve and build it. You might have seen people who have limited themselves on the extent of performance; those already have a perspective of "I can't change."

An example of someone with a fixed mindset is one who believes that he is an athlete because he can sprint to some extent. The mindset would be known during training sessions. If he insists that he can't break the track record but can only maintain his current streak of performance, then he is susceptible to be one.

The fixed mindset does not see opportunities to get better at what they do, and they put no effort to improve. You may have come across people who are dogmatic about using some modern facilities just because they were raised by their grandparents, and must have been misinformed. Whenever there is any change, then it is not for them.

Also, consider when a student is taught how to solve a particular problem in Mathematics. If the facilitator adds variables to the question, then explaining it conventionally becomes a problem (something a fixed mindset will give up on because he felt the other way around is the best way to solve it), so, he gives up.

He could have accepted his weakness in not knowing the problem and then looked for a way around it. The change in the question posed a threat to him already, and he felt helpless, and that was enough reason to give up. If he were asked why he gave up, it would be easy to point fingers, go defensive, and retaliate.

The Growth Mindset

A growth mindset accommodates changes to improve skills and qualities through perseverance, dedication, and effort. People with this mindset believe in all-around development by building strengths and abilities, not just where they feel they have the ability.

These people have an understanding that learning can be developed with persistence. Although when failure comes, it is with an understanding that it can get better, and not an avenue to shy away. They have an insight into the realities of possibilities.

People with a growth mindset are most likely to work at their full potential because challenges do not make them stop, but instead put in more effort. For example, one out of five foreign students in a German class has difficulties in the language. A growth mindset will not get discouraged because he didn't meet the standard of others, but will understand that he just needs to give more effort. Patience will be another thing to take note of here.

5 Tips for Developing a Mindset That Brings You Success

1. Create a Platform to Learn Something Different Every Day

The dependency of fixed traits will not breed a world-class result. Take time to speak with a professional in the line of your strength and ability. There is always a better version of your power. The expert should be able to guide you effectively and push you to do the right thing at every needed moment. Take the pain of learning and doing something different from your immediate talent every day. You may also consider reading about what you learn online or join a friend who wants to learn the same with you

2. Expand your Learning Experience

It is super cool to hear of one's assessment from people. But when it becomes a habit, then you need to be wary. You don't have to focus on getting approval from people around you. It does not matter what they think or say about what you do. Channel that energy into learning. Learning should be your priority and follow the procedures patiently. Bear in mind also that education is a process, and it may not come easy as you would expect. The learning experience will keep you going to achieve great results.

3. Reference Weakness

You must know where the problem is coming from. It might be triggers or just your community of friends. Enough of the excuses for failure and dejection! Embrace your weakness by acknowledging it. This will be the first step in liberating yourself to the world of growth.

4. Be Open to Different Eventualities

Challenges would definitely come, but you have to be prepared for it. Prepare your mind to see the goodness in every difficulty. Learn to weigh your options. Always consider using "what if." You might have decided to read for three hours a day, and it seems unachievable. Ask questions and challenge your routine. What if I have not been following my guide? What if I need to be more specific? What if I need to take breaks? What if I check my diet? What if I read about people who have done the same thing?

5. Reflect Daily

You should be in charge of disbursing the truth to yourself. Have time to meditate on your course of action. You might find it interesting to do this at night when you are done with the work for the day. Analyze those thoughts that have limited you to underperform and how you can overcome them.

CHAPTER THREE: GETTING THE JOB DONE

Productivity entails a lot of things, and one of the most important of them is about getting things done. As easy as it may look, a lot of people still have problems getting things done at the right time and in a complete manner.

This is where the understanding of productivity comes into play. To be productive is to understand tips and techniques and know-how to apply them accordingly. Productivity works like a system, but it doesn't just go into action.

In this chapter, I will be guiding you through some of these factors that can help you become more productive. The techniques and tips I will be revealing to you will yield viable results for you if only you decide to use them unflinchingly.

11 Essential Techniques to Power Up Your Productivity

To understand ways to build productivity, it is necessary that one understands the meaning of productivity. They are many misconceptions about the term, and if they are not handled, the whole essence of this chapter will never be accomplished.

First of all, bear it in mind that productivity isn't only about ticking boxes off your to-do list. It is more than that. Productivity, in this sense, basically entails getting the right things done in the right time frame in the most effective way possible. Having the perfect system to help you boost productivity is very necessary for both your work life and your family life. You definitely stay ahead of things when you understand the mechanisms that fuel productivity.

The building blocks of productivity is in setting up realistic goals and achieving them one step at a time. At the end of the task, you should be able to ask yourself, "Did I do something meaningful with the space of time allocated to me?" If the answer is yes, then congratulations are in order. You have been productive.

One major reason why people fail at being productive is that they have too much going on for them. Being able to select the right task for you and going after them headlong is a very special and important skill that you should learn. There a whole lot more techniques that are quite important when trying to become more productive, and I am going to walk you through some of them. Follow these techniques closely, and watch productivity take a great leap in your life.

1. **The Eisenhower Matrix**

You will most definitely need a pen and paper for these techniques because you will have to draw out a quadrant. The first two quadrants at the top of the four squares will be tagged "very important." The next two underneath will be tagged "less important." But the first two quadrants from the left side will be tagged "urgent" while the next two quadrants at the right will be tagged "less urgent."

After that is complete, you can now begin to sort all your tasks into the boxes. There are those that will fall under "very important" but "less urgent." Others will be "very urgent" but "less important." It is all about understanding how to place each task. Every task that falls into "very important" and "very urgent" should be the ones that you will face quickly. Those definitely carry a lot of weight. On the other hand, those that fall into "less urgent" and "less important" are the ones that can be left for later. Assigning your tasks in all of these boxes will help you with your decision making.

2. The 80/20 rule

The idea of the 80/20 rule comes from a business model. What it means is that 80% of all your profits come from lesser than 20% of your customers and business partners. With that, it is necessary that you know how to treat this 20 % so that they stay and keep providing you with 80% of your profit.

Bring that into your daily life and see how it translates. Notice how just a few things you do actually have a lot of impact on your life. Less than 20% of your everyday activities are enough to have a real influence on your life over a long period of time. It would make sense to place a strong focus on that 20 % so that more meaningful impact can be generated.

3. The Five Majors

This concept was developed by the CEO of Stack Overflow, and its concepts encourage that one person should never have more than five activities on their to-do list at any point in time. Keep your lists short and try to achieve everything on the list with a short period so that you can add more activities to the list and go ahead. You should be working on at least two activities on your list, the next two should be in a queue, and the last one should be a secret task that only you know about, something you must have challenged yourself to do.

4. Exercise your Body and Mind

Exercise frees your body and gets it ready to perform. Exercise in this form does not only have to do with the body alone but also the mind. While the body profits from your physical exercise, the mind profits from mental exercise. Mental exercise helps you to open up your mind and allow your imaginations to run wild, which is quite beneficial to your productivity.

5. A Break will Help you

Some of the most productive people understand the power of breaks. Not only will they help your body relax and feel out new ways to relax and get things done, but they will also allow your mind to re-strategize plans. Have you noticed how the best ideas come to you when you have totally forgotten about the job? Yes, that is your brain working on its own, undisturbed by the stress of your coaxing and anxious mind. Instead of working for long stretches, set a timer and get things done in little bits. They will cumulate into one big success story.

6. Shun Multitasking

There are people who have optimized their bodies and minds for multitasking. It is quite easy for them. That is rarely ability, too. No one is saying you can learn it now, but don't gamble with it just yet. Take time to study yourself and find out how good you are with multitasking. Chances are, you are not very good; so it will be best for you not to venture there. Nothing kills productivity faster than a person trying to multitask. And in the real sense of things, multitasking is a form of distraction in itself. Your mind remains divided throughout the process. Just focus on one job at a time and see how far you can go with that.

7. Love the Things you Do

This is not easy to do, especially for people who have found themselves in jobs that they are not happy with. If you are not happy, then it means you do not love what you do, which leads to frustration. If you are not happy, it is better you leave and find something that gives you fulfillment. The truth is that you can hardly be productive doing something you do not love. If you love it, your mind will no longer view it as work, and it will be easier for you to perform the said tasks.

8. Strangle your Distractions

Getting rid of glaring distractions is key to increasing productivity. Every entertainment in your life is there to reduce your productivity level. Once you understand that and deal with them squarely, it will be easier to overcome them as they arrive. Tell your mind to focus on the essentials and not look sideways to the non-essentials. The funny thing is that your mind obeys you, and it, too, would like to see a specific task completed.

Find a quiet place where you can work, a place where you are sure you will not be distracted. This is the first step in dealing with distractions. If you have created a list, then tell yourself that there will be no fun for you until you have accomplished about three things on that list. Breaking our tasks into smaller bits always helps.

9. Complete the Most Important Tasks First Thing in the Morning

The best time to complete your most intimidating tasks is early in the morning when your mind is most vibrant and ready to perform. Don't put off your task until it becomes late, and then you find yourself rushing the task to complete the task. Begin before your mind starts to slack and watch yourself progress even before the day goes halfway. Completing the most taxing activities early in the morning will give your mind and body a kind of positive push to keep trying harder.

10. Create a Schedule

Don't just rush into things without a plan. A schedule will help you to streamline your activities and keep you more focused while helping to eliminate distractions. But don't forget to create time for rest and pleasure in your schedule. If not, it will never be a workable one. Take off whole hours to get yourself together and replenish your mind.

11. Reward yourself

If you have achieved anything that marks you off as productive, then you should reward yourself. Your reward can come in any form, but make sure it is something you will enjoy, something you will thank yourself for. Having rewards set in place will give you something to look forward to asking you try to complete the task as fast as possible.

10 Secrets Behind Productivity According to the World's Billionaires

There is no better place to get advice than from the best of the best, some of the most productive people in the world who are billionaires. It is not easy to control your environment, but you can learn how to do so, and this is something that billionaires are quite good at. You should sit down and try to learn from them.

The world has more than 1500 billionaires, and most of them are quite effective at time management and productivity. Don't get it twisted. These people live the same kind of lives as you. They receive thousands of emails every day that require sorting. They have thousands of employees in their payrolls, and they also have a lot of decisions to make every day. Have you ever wondered how they manage to stay on top and achieve so much in such little time? How they choose the things that are important and those that can be left for a later time? These are men and women who have built their wealth systems in such a way that they receive in excess of $5000 every day. And productivity is something they don't joke with.

Here are some of the most outlined points that they listed as some of their most important:

1. You Don't Have to be Everywhere

The late Steve Jobs stated that to increase his productivity; he spent a lot of time streamlining the number of meetings and places he had to be per day. Some other billionaires stated that there is no need to attend a meeting or being in a place if you are sure that you won't make a lot of money from it, or talk about something really important. It is more important that you delegate someone to go on your behalf instead of presenting yourself at the venue. Most high-profile billionaires have described most meetings as a waste of time with people talking about irrelevant things.

2. Simplify your Calendar

Your calendar here refers to your schedule. Most billionaires advise that people learn to keep their calendar simple and decongested. Instead of having hundreds of things to be done in one week, try picking out a select few to be accomplished within that week and leave the rest for the next week. It is no good trying to stuff your schedule with lots of things and not achieving any of them in the long run.

3. Identify the Place Where you Perform Best

We are all different, and we all have different psychologies. Because of this, the areas where we most liable to perform best differ from person to person. Find your place and stick to it. What time of the day do you perform best? How should a surrounding be before you can get in the zone to work? For some people, a loud and noisy environment is the ideal place to work. For others, it will be a silent and very secluded environment where they will come in contact with very few people.

Once you find out what works best for you, build on it and enhance that environment. Some billionaires have thinking rooms built into their homes where they sit and think for hours on end; others travel to very secluded places where they can commune better with themselves. And all of these produce very wonderful results for different individuals, especially when they are practiced in the right way.

4. Keep your Focus on the Most Important Goals

There are goals, and there are GOALS. The key here is not allowing other less important goals to hold you back from achieving the main important goals. People who achieve a lot know how to set the most important goals and face them like their lives depend on it. This is not to say that you ignore your other dreams. Instead, keep your eyes on the big ones, those ones that will have the most positive impact in your life within the shortest time.

5. How Well are you Doing?

Billionaires are people that love to track their process on any project. Nothing is ever done just because it is done. They live their life intentionally and love to follow all of those intentions and see success. It is advised that you create metrics with which you can use to determine how good you are performing. Your metrics can be using a small book to write down everything you achieve or making use of software or apps that help to track process. With a fully tracked process, you will be able to look and improve your performances.

6. Take Advantage of all the People Around you

The people around you are some of your most important resources. It is quite neglected, but billionaires have always advised people to be more conscious of the people around them. If you are the kind of person who loves to work on your own and shut out other people, then you should learn to make some adjustments in your life. People are always around that can make your life more successful, and you should maximize them. Billionaires basically report that they recruit people to help them achieve their dreams and ideas. Getting to use people is to create more time for yourself. The job gets faster in a shorter time. The major problem is in finding competent people; but once you are able to scale that, you will have the most productive time of your life.

7. Technology is There for you

Renowned billionaires around the world are known for their love of technology. Look what Facebook did for Zuckerberg. Look at Steve Jobs, Bill Gates, and other selected ones. Sometimes technology is your best option. Technology gets it done easier and quicker.

Automation can work in any business as long as you are able to discover a way to introduce it into your business to help you work better. All you have to do is make sure you already have an efficiently working system before you incorporate technology into your work. If not, you might end up confusing yourself and achieving nothing.

8. Create habits that help your Productivity

Billionaires are people of practice; they know how to build positive habits that help them to become more productive. Some of them are known to be early morning people; others are known to be nocturnal animals. Billionaires know how to develop the perfect habits to help them out to become more productive.

9. Set Time for the Most Important Work

Remember that activity is not equal to productivity. Don't allow yourself to get drowned in the hustle and bustle of life. There should be a set time for you to carry out the most tasking of your activities. Productive billionaires know that special time needs to be set aside to get the most important jobs done. During this time, there will be no calls, no emails, and no internet. It will be only you and the job right there in front of you.

10. Recognize your Opportunities

Productive billionaires unsurprisingly have the best eyes suited for figuring the best opportunities that should be maximized. You will be tempted to take on every viable opportunity in front of you, but not all opportunities are for you. Take time to review all the opportunities in front of you and find the ones that best suit your skills and personality.

5 Time Management Strategies to get More Done in Less Time

There is something about time management you need to know: Time cannot be managed. Instead, you can only manage the events that occur within a period of time, giving the illusion that time has been managed. Every one of us has been provided with the same quantity of time, which is 24 hours per day and 7 days per week and so on. So, the question now is, how can you fit all of your activities into this period of time so that you come out with the utmost satisfaction and remain productive?

With this understanding, it is also necessary that you note that time is also a commodity. It can be sold and it can be bought. It can also be budgeted, and it can be used with wisdom and common sense. Another thing is that time management is an art that can be mastered.

Time management strategies are affected by different factors when they are applied by different individuals. Personality, will to achieve, and the level of discipline are some of the factors that can affect a person's ability to manage time. These strategies have been proven over time to help people with managing their time. Practice them and watch your life change.

1. Be Organized

Disorganization and poor time management go hand-in-hand. Where one is present, the other manifests itself. Get rid of any form of clutter that may have besieged your life so that time will be spent more wisely.

There are simple ways in which you can achieve organization and a decluttered life. There are thousands of resources on the internet that can help you out, but the simple way out is to learn when to let go of things. Know what to put away and what to leave. Note that the clutter that is being referred to does not only have to do with the physical everyday clutter. There is also the mental clutter and digital clutter. All of these have a way of slowing you down and reduce your ability to manage time.

To get rid of mental clutter, make sure that your mind stays clear both emotionally and psychologically. An unstable mind is a distraction, which in turn deprives you of focus. Digital clutter, on the other hand, will mix up your files that will make you spend hours looking for a document. Deal with all of these individually and return your life to stability.

2. Identify and Deal with Time Wasters

Your productivity and time management is affected by a lot of external factors controlled by the people and circumstances in your life at any given moment. These factors are some of the major causes of time wastage, as they have a way of affecting you without your knowledge. All that happens is that with time, you discover that you missed something somewhere. But you have the power to either increase or decrease their effect such that they are no longer capable of wasting your precious time. Some of these factors you should look out for include:

- Uninvited visitors or guests
- Unimportant emails and letters to be replied
- The internet (social media)
- Relationships
- Little pleasures

3. Is your Time Worth Anything?

Take a few minutes and try to take stock of your time. How much is it worth to you? If it is worth something, then how can it translate into productivity? Once you do this, you will find for yourself a sense of understanding that your time should be spent wisely because of its worth. When the value of a thing is unidentified, it is easy for it to be abused and misused. Create value for your time and don't allow that value to ever be reduced. If you are going to get distracted for 15 minutes, you should be able to determine how much you must have lost during those gone 15 minutes. With that in place, you will easily be able to organize your mind and get yourself to act.

4. Care for Yourself

Taking care of yourself is one major way in which you can avoid time wastage. Take time to relax your body, your mind, and your soul. Keeping your body and mind at its best helps you accomplish tasks even faster than usual. Find out what time of your day your body performs best and maximize those periods to the best of your ability.

Mismanagement of time can manifest as a result of bodily fatigue and sickness. Depression can also cause you to put off important activities, and this is why your mental health should also be checked from time to time. As I have noted before, take time to rejuvenate your mind and reward yourself whenever you are sure you have accomplished something noteworthy.

There should be a healthy balance in your life between your work and family. There can never be any form of real productivity without this balance in place. Instead, you will spend a lot of time thinking you are productive at work while your personal life experiences failure.

5. A Necessary Sense of Urgency

To have a sense of urgency is to understand that there is no room for time wastage. It is to understand that speed is necessary when an opportunity presents itself. Develop the ability to take action and to take them very quickly. It is one thing to take the corresponding action, and it is another to take that action before it becomes too late. One thing that differentiates achievers from their opposites is their ability to take appropriate action sat the right time.

CHAPTER FOUR: SHARPENING FOCUS

Awareness is a thing to remember when learning to get focused, whether on personal targets or on assigned duties. It is one of the tools leaders consider in achieving a massive turnout of success. The beginning of this consciousness positions leaders to direct the attention of people following them. To sustain this growth, the leader must focus on their care.

We must first know that getting focused is beyond filtering alternatives while paying attention to one. One could concentrate in diverse ways and for different purposes to pursue an available course. Being a leader here does not necessarily mean you lead in a position of authority, and you are not pushed to the thought of being one. Our priority is to ensure that you lead a proper life for yourself.

Remember that there is a larger world to give attention to; those things that connect you to the world. People following you (comprising of people you work with or for, the ones you mentor, and the ones you are accountable for) deserves attention too, and lastly, yourself.

Problems you complain of often might come from distraction, or maybe multitasking. With things ranging from meetings to work schedule, back-to-back reviews and presentations, and finally again to supervision, note how each day has become a mountain of workload. And you could barely have time to sort out your thoughts. This schedule would be reasonable if you are 100% sure of your success rate and might not need a rethink. But in the long run, you might break down both mentally and physically.

14 EXERCISES TO DEVELOP RAZOR-SHARP FOCUS

We would begin with those little daily tasks you often consider as of little importance. Expect to see a change as you hold the exercises with the utmost value. This mind will be the breakthrough to sustain the success of the activities.

1. **Learn your Work Structure**
   Increase your focus rate by understanding the details of the job. Ask questions on what is unclear. Meet your supervisor or your direct superior and make clarifications. You might want to ask for a record of such a task that has been done before. Your inquisitiveness would clear the doubt that would have misled you. And will only make you look out for the excellent completion of the job. Your focus would now be sharpened as you can now comprehend every fragment of your work schedules.

2. **Arrange your Desk**
   This exercise will deal with every distraction that might spring from clutter. Imagine your table is full of unfinished reports, seminar papers, minutes, and other relevant official documents. What happens is any time you see them gives you anxiety and worry. Fear tends to creep in.

   Instead of allowing such unnecessary pressure from your mind, arrange or rearrange your desk as the case may be. Keep documents in their order of priority and gain some peace for your mind, if for nothing else. This action will allow you to be conscious of what is most significant at the moment, and you will be mindful of it.

3. **Stretch your Body**
   Mental capability is not isolated from our physical components. Your hands, leg, even neck plays a lot of role in improving your productivity level. Note that I am not negating other parts of your body; neither do I underestimate their functions. Our attention here is the role each of your locomotive parts plays in revitalizing your body.

   Practice twisting your fingers one after the other in a clockwise rotation. You need to be careful and gentle with this exercise so as not to injure yourself. Continue the rotation for five minutes and pay attention to the steady movement you are making. Fix your mind on all you notice, starting from the sound of the first two rotations to the unequal flow of the tip bone. You might see your veins and how your wrist tends to move with the spinning finger. Take time to do this with all your fingers with your mind focusing on the movement.

   You might extend this practice to your hand, too. Stretch and keep your hand still for about 12 seconds and fix your gaze at the outstretched arm. You might want to try other parts of your body too. Just ensure that you pay attention to all you do.

4. **A Three-Minute Study of an Insect**
   Insects are almost everywhere. Good places to enjoy this exercise will be in your garden and at a park. Take a walk to a park and sit under a tree. Look closely at the bark of the tree. You would surely see an insect. It might be on the grass or at the branches of a flower/plant. Any one you notice first is good to go with.

   Get close to the tree or plant but not too close; make sure you look around closely so as not to disturb other insects. Study the movement of the insect(s). Put close attention to where they started their journey. You might be fortunate enough to see them carry particles (if walking with their friends and neighbors) from one place to another.

Your focus will improve if you could pick one insect out of many and use your sight to monitor it for 3 minutes. This period of mindfulness might look long to you because of their movement, resemblance, body structure, and color.

5. **Colored Bottle Study**

    All you need for this exercise are different-colored bottles. You can have a mix of plastic and ceramic jars. Place them on a table and create a little distance from it. Stare at them as long you can. Start with three different colors which might be a mix of your favorite. You might tend to focus more on one color than on others; your aim is to be mindful of a specific color. The more you are aware of your choice bottle, the more your focus is strengthened.

    Whenever your mind wanders away from your task, try to bring it back as quickly as possible. You may also want to write down those thoughts that flash through your mind during the process of this exercise.

6. **Jazz Music Break Down**

    The genre of this music might not be your pick but listening to it will help boost your focus level. Notice that there is a soft combination of musical instruments for this kind of music. Your attention should be on the timing of each of the instruments used.

    Your first assignment is to get into the rhythm. How does music make you feel? Your present environment is not your concern for now, and that's why it will be best for you to do this exercise behind closed doors. The next thing to do is to channel your emotions to your thought. To do this, bring your feelings to align with your ideas through the music. There is an emotion that follows the piano, while the drum set is different also. Just flow with the music and don't wander away.

7. **Smell Exercise**
This exercise will work well for those who have a strong sense of smell. But it doesn't leave out every other person. Every time there is a strong smell, try and be a detective. Exert effort to trace where the smell is coming from. It might be the smell of a coffee, perfume, flower, or even food. Let your brain interpret the scent and enjoy the feeling they bring to you. You might go further to know the intensity as in the case of food. You might want to determine whenever the food is boiling or burning.

8. **Movie Report**
Your kind of movie might be romance or action. Your focus on film should be on how well you can tell another person about the most exciting part. If you can do this successfully, then move a step higher by becoming the movie to talk about to a friend. Doing this will require more serious attention than the movie. You are both the actor and director here. Detailed and specific information will be required on all you do and how you do them. This exercise will allow you to comprehend your actions and will most likely expose the intent behind them.

9. **Feel your Pulse**
No tool will be required to carry out this exercise. For you to be successful on this one, you first need to monitor how you breathe. Put attention on how you inhale and exhale. At what rate? And under what conditions do you breathe either fast or slow? You might notice that when you are a bit anxious, your breathing changes compared to when you are confident.

Be in a comfortable position, either on the floor or chair. Make sure your body is relaxed. Take a slow, but deep breath and launch into the experience. Focus on the subtle sound of your pulse and breathe. You might also want to experience how slowly your chest expands.

The attention given at first might not be as perfect as a golden plantain. Don't be hard on yourself. Do it repeatedly and enjoy the tranquillity that accompanies the natural thought pattern of this exercise.

10. See with your Eyes Closed

Since the eye is the organ than gives sight, it is the most accessible doorway to most distractions. We don't need to pluck out those eyes to stop seeing them. But we can also rely on it to strengthen our focus.

Go to a public place but with few people around, close your eyes, and focus on your feelings. If you are successful in combining your emotions well, step further in this exercise by going to where there is a crowd. Notice the sounds around you — the footsteps, chant, and chat. Can you still concentrate on your feelings? If yes, then try as much as possible to understand what is going on around you. Once you get to this level, your mindfulness has increased to a definite high.

11. Conscious Listening

This exercise is similar to the movie report, only the group of friends involved is different. Speak to your friends about having a heart-to-heart discussion. It will be interesting if you have a mix of males and females.

Group yourselves into groups of two from opposite sexes and form a listening clique. Ensure there is a coordinator that monitors this exercise. Discuss any subject you all agree to converse with friends only. When your partner is done, switch roles and be the one to listen. Timing will be necessary for this exercise, say five minutes. When the clique is done with their first ten minutes, the coordinator then announces for both of you to share each other's story as you heard it. Ensure that you use the exact word, phrase, and possibly the gesture as you were told. Make your partner's story appear personal to you.

At the end of everyone's session, the coordinator then allows everyone to comment on their experience. At the end of this game, everyone would have been able to achieve some level of strengthened attention.

12. Conscious Eating

Conscious eating here does not mean impulse eating or feeding, influenced by emotions. It entails the awareness needed when eating your daily meals. And since food is essential for our daily nutritional needs, we could both enjoy the feelings attached to it through mindfulness. The satisfaction will come when you have an understanding of why you eat. The thought of the reason should be far from hunger. It's about building a relationship with food.

Let's start with the process of cooking and the smell attached to it. Maybe you have not been conscious enough to absorb the feelings attached to "pre-cooking and pre-eating." Your aim when eating shouldn't be to swallow. What about the coloring, the garnishing, and cutlery arrangement?

Enjoy your next meal by taking it in bits. Bite, steadily chew the food, and allow yourself to experience the feeling of each spoon.

While eating, you may ask yourself if the emotion attached to it is right. Don't eat because everyone seems to be eating at that moment. You have likely been doing this before, but you might not enjoy this exercise if that is what motivates you to eat. Remember that our aim for this exercise is to be able to concentrate on every detail of what you eat.

13. Conscious sitting and standing

We often do this without taking into account how frequently we do this. It will best describe acute mindfulness if you account for your daily activities. Sitting and standing is one that could boost laser focus ability. One is likely to rise and rest many times in a day without taking cognizance of it. Your job requirement might force you to do so.

But you could also build mindfulness in doing the same. Be in charge of the decision to either stand or sit. It might not sound easy at first, but it's worth the try, and you may even remember after you have walked a few meters. Once you register this consciousness as a new vocabulary in your mind, you will see yourself getting familiar with it.

14. Word Count Exercise

Try this exercise with your favorite book, magazine or newspaper. Start with five paragraphs and read them. After you must have absorbed the content, begin the word count. Count each word from the first paragraph to the last and repeat the process in descending order. It will be essential for you to note each word you count. Keep to memory the usage, function, and intent. The more you do the counting, the more you are aware of the words.

You could also commit to mind the number of words in each paragraph. When you are sure of your achievement for five sections, you can proceed to 10, 20, or even a whole chapter.

The Crucial Link Between your Brain and your Belly

One crucial factor to consider when thinking of a healthy lifestyle is the food you take. The traditional benefits of food spans from medicinal to nutritional; it is the most considered build-up to all-around soundness of the body. As it is said, "You are what you eat."

Individual meals are prescribed to patients based on their illness, imperfections, and symptoms. And this has proven to be effective over time. Asides genetic factors, feeding has the capability to change the growth level of individuals. An example will be a comparison between well-fed children to malnourished ones.

There is a connection between our productivity level and the food we eat. You would agree that not eating adequately has a way of telling on the brain. Remember when you were famished; it was as if nothing is working in you. The only thought that filled your mind is the consumption of food. This feeling is not strange because the presence or absence of food has been proven to regulate your activeness, alertness, energy, and willingness. When you're hungry, your ability to focus was reduced, and your mood was not at its best.

Your brain suffers when you are hungry because it can't perform to its highest potential. You won't be able to focus on a task; and even when you do, it is most likely not to be excellent because your blood sugar level is not regulated.

1. **Almonds**
   This fruit contains fiber and protein, which are known to increase feelings of fullness. Eating this nut allows you to consume fewer calories per day. It also has an antioxidant called

phytic acid which protects against oxidative stress. Ensure you consume the brown layer of the skin

2. **Salmon**
The presence of high omega-3 fatty acids content is what makes salmon able to boost memory and mental performance. You might not get disappointed quickly. A fish oil supplement can also achieve optimum results for depression.

3. **Green Tea**
This natural tea contains L-Theanine. This property is a component that increases calmness and tranquillity. It works perfectly with another part called caffeine by making it release steadily. Caffeine boosts focus and alertness. You could stay active all day when you enjoy it in its powdery form.

4. **Bananas**
Banana contains glucose which releases energy to the body. Eating a banana a day will complement the daily need for glucose. It is also great as a between-meals food as it will fill you up. You may try it with a peanut for a composed snack and experience the refreshing moment all day. The presence of pectin in banana regulates blood sugar level and reduces appetite by reducing the vastness of the stomach

5. **Eggs**
An egg contains an abundance of Omega-3 fat and a B-vitamin called choline, among other nutrients. It works to enhance the mental reactive sensors and also raises the High-density lipoprotein which is connected to reduce the possibilities of many diseases

The nutrient in egg appears more as one of its calories is higher than most foods. These nutrients can help to keep the hunger away for an extended period.

6. **Brown Rice**
The magnesium present in brown rice relieves stress and boosts productivity. Unlike white rice, the energy present is released slowly to increasingly build-up power throughout the day. The

health benefit is contained in its whole grain form. Another fantastic component is the low glycemic index. The glycemic index shows how fast a food raises a person's blood sugar. Brown rice is rated as an average GI food making it easy to consume.

7. **Dark Chocolate**

   Once the concentration of cocoa is 70 percent or higher in chocolate, then the nutritional value is a thing to celebrate. The flavonoids found in chocolate as well as in other fruits and vegetables has an anti-allergic, anti-inflammatory, and anti-tumor properties. Flavonols also reduce the risk of heart disease, cancer, and stoke. It seeks to lower blood pressure and helps in blood flow, leaving your body active all day. Once your heart is perfect, your brain wouldn't have any issues functioning.

8. **Blueberries**

   Blueberries are noted for its antioxidant properties that fight disease, as well as able to stop belly bloat. The hidden benefit of this fruit is that it enhances cognitive ability. Your brain is set for the day with this fruit

5 Ways to Develop Unwavering Self-Discipline

Learning does not stop at the moment of doing; it continues until the behavior is personalized. You wouldn't approve of a child's knowledge until it becomes part of the child's way of life. For example, after a child has learned cleanliness in school but still litters his room with toys, you would agree that he has not applied the knowledge to his daily life. The assertion might not be accurate if he keeps a clean room in the first week of learning but fails to continue after the following weeks. It is not because of failed memory; it is due to a lack of desire, drive, and motivation to persist. We can generally say that he is not disciplined enough to continue.

Self-discipline entails every effort to control yourself. This definition might sound vague as you feel that you have always been in charge of your decisions. It might be correct, but what about your impulses, emotions, and feelings? Those are the big cards of your successes and failures, depending on how well you have mastered the game. The ability to consciously commit yourself to fulfill your goals irrespective of varying feelings can be termed self-discipline.

By now, you must have improved your level of focus. Sustaining this achievement is why self-discipline is necessary as this will form another habit in you. The process will not be a fast one but will surely help your productivity level and sustain any of your learned positive behavior.

It will begin with a steady approach to carefully analyze what you do in line with becoming better. For example, trying the conscious listening exercise will allow you to adapt to the changing conditions of different sounds in your environment, and allows you to flow with the circumstance without affecting your mindfulness (inner self).

An acute understanding of this subject will help you to achieve an excellent result to maintain a top-notch focus, beat laziness, and defeat procrastination. Take to heart the following nuggets to sustained self-discipline:

1. **Identify and Analyze your Triggers**
   Positioning yourself in a safe zone is not only necessary when involved in a hazardous task; it should be natural. Our helmet here is to sustain self-discipline is to identify the triggers that cause distraction. This action is not only aimed at achieving success alone but digging deep to the root to measure the cause of its repeated failure. What causes you to lose focus? What are those factors that push you to perform the task in the future?

Do a proper assessment of those elements and be sincere as much as possible. The same thing goes to those triggers that increase your productivity level. It is possible to have the same factor contributing to both increased productivity and procrastination. For example, your partner at your workplace might inspire you to do more through his unrelenting attitude to work, and at the same time, make you an addict to the digital world.

Once you are clear on your triggers, propose alternative options to scale through. Try to write them down. It may involve the same way you write your to-do-list. Create another not-to-do-list to counter those issues. Through this approach, you won't see yourself falling into the same pit time and again.

2. **Be Sure of Your Purpose**
A strong desire to win will be required to maintain an unwavering self-discipline course. Ask a series of questions. Why do I want to read a chapter of a book a day? Why must I eat cereal once in every two days? Self-awareness is necessary to keep you going. Analyze your feelings and emotions to be sure that you are not playing on them. Have a clarity that your pre-learned behavior is not on a temporary assumption or influenced by the rhythm of the moment.

3. **Build a Motivation Block**
Create a system that will continuously fuel your passion to commitment. It might be a competitive environment where you can outwork or outperform others. Since you can measure your progress with hardworking colleagues, your progress will be on track.
Another motivation block can be to introduce a reward-and-punishment tool. The reward tool might be to buy an item for yourself every time you achieve or surpass a target. It might also

be to take a time-out to have fun. You might think of paying a friend an agreed sum of money as your punishment tool. Just ensure that your motivation is keeping you going.

4. **Choose a Model**

   Look to the outside world to keep on track. Search for someone who has been on the path you want to tread. He/she should be someone who has mastered the habit and have proven to develop over time. He might be your college professor, your gym instructor, or your spiritual head. Be sure you are right on whom to choose. Get ready to follow whatever you are told to do. It might look rigorous at first, but the desired outcome will surface.

5. **Design a Strategy**

   Here is one of the essential tools to maintain self-discipline: Develop a plan to work with. Discipline is not automatic as it involves a process of building. Your action must comprise of a deadline and an achievable step-to-step guide. The good thing about these mini milestones is that you will be able to measure your progress. And a sound reward system can keep you focused and master an active control system.

   The aim of this plan is not to get overwhelmed by your goals. Progress is the primary fuel that will push you farther to actualize your strategies. Deadlines also will force you to gather all resources at your reach to achieve success on a specific date.

CHAPTER FIVE: GOAL SETTING FOR SUCCESS

You may have spent a lot of time wondering why things don't just seem to work out well for you. One time you have a dream burning in your mind with full plans to accomplish that dream, and the next thing you know, it is gone, and you have accomplished nothing. You may have also spent a lot of time in thoughts, comparing yourself with people who achieve things with ease; people who it seems were simply born to be successful. These people know what they want, state what they want, and follow it with all their zeal until they see it achieved.

There is little or no secret attached to these people and their success. The only thing that differentiates you from them is the ability to set goals. These people don't only work hard; they work smart. And working smart entails setting strong and workable goals. Without goals, life would simply be directionless, and a directionless life will be an unproductive life with nothing to live for.

Most of the time, only a few of us sit down and chart a course for our lives. Take life like a stormy sea, with you and your boat floating on that sea. There is every possibility of you being taken off course. But if you have a compass, it will be easier for you to find your way home after the storm has subsided. Your goal is like a compass that helps to put you back in check after a period of going astray.

In this chapter, we will be going through some of the basics of setting goals. What are the best techniques and tips that you should employ while setting goals? How realistic and workable should your goals be so that they don't end up frustrating you as you work towards achieving them?

Concepts Associated with Goal Setting

Before we begin to explore the necessary techniques for goal setting, there are some concepts about goal setting that you have to understand. If these are not well-understood, then I tell you that the whole process will end up filled with failure. The most important question of all is:

> **Why do I need to set goals?** This is a very personal question, and you would need to provide a personal answer before you can go on. Without providing an answer, you will never be able to connect with the goal-setting activity on a more personal level.

In setting goals, these two things will help you out in forging something that works.

- **What are your goals?** What exactly is it that you want? Do you want to land on the moon someday? Do you need to lose more than 100 pounds with 6 months? Are you planning to win an Oscar before you turn 40? Identify these goals because they will provide you with instant clarity. The goals will help your mind as a compass to accomplishment. In fact, an identified goal sets your heart on fire like no other.
- **Why do you want to accomplish these goals?** I can't tell you anything more important in goal setting. Without a purpose or a reason, your goals are as good as nuts. Take some time off and evaluate your reason for setting these goals? Do you need to get a good car so it would help you feel good around your peers or because it will help you move faster around town? Are you trying to lose weight because someone insulted you about your plus-size or because you simply want to live healthier? As you may know, a goal set for a selfish reason never gets to see the light of day as regards its achievement. With a concrete and

well-laid purpose, your goal setting will be a whole lot more easily.

Forms of Goals

To effectively set a goal, you need to understand what kind of goal you are setting. There are different types and finding the right one will help you a long way. The most important form of goal categorization is the one that is done based on the timeline. These include:

1. **Short-Term Goals:** These goals are those that can be achieved in a short time, say within a period of six months or less than a year. When setting such goals, you should look at those that can be easily achieved so that you can go forward with the next goal.
2. **Long-Term Goals:** These goals take a longer space of time before they fully actualized. They even take years. Some of these goals make include learning and starting up a business, raising a child, or beating cancer.
3. **Lifelong Goals:** Goals like these may take you a lifetime to accomplish. The thing with lifelong goals is that you may never know when they will be accomplished. At some point, you are bound to get frustrated and want to give up. But you should note that lifelong goals as built on the achievement of long-term and short-term goals. A goal example of a lifelong goal is a child with a dream of becoming the President.

10 Goal-Setting Techniques to Achieve your Goals Faster

1. Identify the Benefits of Achieving that Goal.

It is one thing for you to know the purpose of following a goal through to the end, and it is a different thing to understand the benefit of achieving that goal. If a goal comes with no benefit, either for you or the people around you, then there will be no need to pursue it because even your mind will feel frustrated trying to compel you to action. Knowing what is in it for you will be enough drive to help you sit up and get to work. For an exercise, pick your goal-setting book and jot down some of the benefits that you will enjoy if a goal is achieved. Think long and hard while filling those spaces with answers.

2. **Set Compatible Goals.**

When trying to set goals you can easily achieve, it is necessary that you make them compatible with each other. Setting incompatible goals make you waste your time and energy. Soon you will find yourself feeling very stressed out and weak, unable to go on with the pursuit of your goals. One goal may be to spend more time with people and make new friends, and another goal may be to learn how to be on your own more often and focus on a given task. These two are conflicting. You can't spend more time with friends and still have enough time to complete the task. When putting down goals, it is necessary that you look into each of them and measure their compatibility with the rest of them on the list.

3. **Create a Standing Balance.**

Don't allow yourself to get too involved in trying to achieve a particular goal that you begin to ignore the others. Life works with balance. You should learn to share your time equally amongst all of your goals. It will make no sense that you succeed in one aspect and fail in the other. You might be experiencing a lot of success in one aspect of your life, but when you discover that the other aspect is unfinished, it might be too late.

4. **Ask for Help When Necessary.**

That is why they are called goals; you can't achieve them alone. There are a lot of people around you who will be willing to help you out with your goals if only you will agree to be humble and meet them. For every goal you may want to achieve, there is someone out there who has achieved that goal a long time ago. You should connect with them and find out how they did it, what obstacles they faced, and how they overcame.

When analyzing your goals, try to identify places in which you can be helped so that you will be more specific in seeking that help. These can include skills you make need to acquire or knowledge to be gotten.

5. **Focus on the Things that will Enhance your Goals.**

When making your schedule for the day, try to basically consider those things that will add value to your goals. Those are the things that you should consider the most. They should take up more of your time. There are other activities that you can modify to help you create more time for these other activities. Do not hesitate to do those.

6. **There is Work to be Done, and No One will Help you Do it.**

This is probably the most important thing you should know about goal setting. It is not just about writing down the goals in a book and staring at them all day long. There is a lot more attached to it, and most of it is work. You should learn to take up the responsibility that will be associated with the work that you are about to do. At some points, if you begin to experience failure, your mind will be eager to help you shift blame. Please overcome this pleasurable temptation. It will lead you nowhere tangible. Instead of allowing yourself to get trapped in the web of complaints and excuses, make up your mind that no matter what happens, that goal must be accomplished.

7. **Do Away with Potential Interruptions and Distractions**

You will encounter a lot of distractions and interruptions on your way to achieving your goals. They will come in many disguises, and parade themselves as things that need to be accomplished urgently.

Perhaps some of them might be legit, so you would need you the discretion to be able to select the wheat from the tares. Most of them will simply be time wasters on a mission to kill your time and slow you down. The ability to successfully differentiate which activities are worth your time is a very important skill you will need to master if you must accomplish those goals.

8. Stay Open to Change

A lot of unexpected things can arise, and you may need to make some changes to your goals. It may be a positive change, but a change all the same. Once you notice that something unplanned and unforeseen is about to take place, that will be the perfect time to make evaluations and know those things that can be changed. You can also keep your mind open and look for opportunities in them.

9. You Will Need a Level of Persistence

Working towards your goal is not all you may need to do to get them to achieve. Putting in all the required effort at the initial stage and then faltering at the end will only make you regret the whole process. Persistence is the necessary spice that makes your hard work pay off. You will surely meet a lot of hard bumps on your way but keeping up with everything required of you is something that will guarantee you success in the long run. Remember that all the things you will be doing now will only be short-term sacrifices, and they will provide you with long-term pleasures. It is up to you.

10. Constantly Review your Goals

Reviewing your goal will help you to identify any progress you may have made over time. It also provides you with the opportunity to pinpoint the places where you may have failed. When reviewing your goals, ask yourself questions about how far you have come achieving the goal, what steps should be changed towards achieving the goal with more speed and if you are still on the right track. Goal review will also help you motivate you towards performing better.

7 Things you Need to Know About Setting the Right Goals

I always tell my audience to find the right goals to set. There are goals for you, and then there are goals that you shouldn't bother setting because they will yield no value to your life. If the right goals are not being set, then there is every possibility of you losing focus even before they are accomplished. Setting the right goals will take some time. The right goals don't just come to you prepared. You might need to brainstorm some ideas before you find which goals are right for you and which aren't. But there are some general techniques you can put in place to help you with your selection. Here are some of them:

1. **The Right Goal can be Measured**

Your goals should be goals that can be easily measured to find out how successful you have been with them. If you write down your goals and break them into bits, then there should be an avenue for you to be able to tick them and measure success. A goal that can be measured should be one that is specific, like, "I will lose ten pounds before the months runs out." or "I should finish writing my next book before the year runs out." All of these are examples of measurable goals. These kinds of goals make it easy for you to track success.

2. **The Right Goals can be Managed**

If you find yourself constantly being overwhelmed by a goal, it may mean that it is not the right goal for you. The right goal is that goal that you can break down into smaller goals. These smaller goals will serve as milestones that will build up to the accomplishment of the main goal. Breaking your goals into smaller bits will help you keep track of its success rate.

3. **The Right Goal can be Achieved No Matter the Hurdles that Come with it**

   Each goal on your goal list must have a point with which you can finally measure success. If your goal does have that point where you can look back and say you have come a long way, then it is an abstract goal. Setting a goal and saying, "I want to sell my products" is not a goal. How many of those products do you want to sell? If you don't clearly define what an achievement is for you, then you won't be able to reward yourself even when you sell a thousand of those products. In your mind, the goal remains unachieved, and soon, you will give up on it. The main thing is to place a target on all your goals.

4. **Any Obstacles Against the Accomplishment of the Right Goals can Easily be Detected a Long Way Off**

   If you run into unforeseen problems while trying to execute a goal, you can take that as a point that the goal wasn't meant for you all along. The right goal is one that allows you to detect any future problems while you are making a review of the steps required to accomplish it. Once these problems present themselves in the initial stage, all you have to do is put in measures to mitigate their effect.

5. **The Right Goal will have a realistic and workable deadline**

   Every goal needs a timeframe, a period with which it should be accomplished. With a set deadline, your mind is moved to work to produce a result. Once you have come up with a timeframe within which your job should be accomplished, you will find out that a sense of urgency will be instantly attached to the job. And having a sense of urgency is something I mentioned earlier, which will help you with your goal-setting venture. There should be enough time that will help you reach the goal, yet the time shouldn't be too long to get you uninterested in the goal. But you should put the magnitude of your goal into consideration when setting a timeframe, so you don't end up deceiving yourself.

6. **The Right Goal can be Easily Visualized**

If you don't have a picture, then you don't have a destination. Does our goal give you a picture? If it does, how tangible and real, is it? When making a review of your goals, picture yourself accomplishing the goal. Picture yourself holding your complete novel in your hands. Picture yourself with your degree in three years' time. Picture yourself in your car. The stronger and clearer the picture, the easier it will be to get the motivation to work towards it. You can easily rejuvenate a dull and unmotivated day by imagining the results of your success. Your goals must have a picture.

7. **The Right Goal will Always Have a Long-Term Value for your Life**

Finally, the right goal is a goal that has rewards that will stay with you for a lifetime. Although there are the right goals with short-lived rewards, most of the right goals always come with rewards that stay longer. When setting each goal, try to analyze and identify the benefits associated with each of them. They may include financial freedom, mental rest, physical health, and psychological stability. Whatever they may be, just know that identifying them will help you a long way.

The Best Ways to Reward Yourself for Completed Goals

First, you have to understand that no one will reward you more than you can reward yourself. You deserve to be rewarded, especially when you have successfully completed a task, herculean or not. Reward your body. Reward your mind. Reward your soul. Reward yourself no matter how little it may be. It definitely goes a long way. To reward yourself is to tell your mind and brain that it has done a good job and will encourage it to do more. Once you can establish this in your mind, you will find out that it will be a lot easier for you to work because your body will be looking forward to that reward received after the first completed job.

To start the process of rewarding yourself, you have to know what the reward will be for. Take out a pen and book and jot down whatever you may want to reward yourself for. Make sure that you have a detailed and comprehensive list before going ahead with the rewarding process. If not, you will only be deceiving yourself. There are many ways for you to reward yourself, and I will introduce you to some of them. But you should also note that your rewards should not come in such a way that they will negate everything you have just worked for. That will be the wrong reward system. The most important things to consider when selecting reward are:

1. **It Should Have Long-Lasting Value**
The reward should be of value to you in any way possible. Don't just go for a reward that will provide you with instant happiness; go for something more concrete and deep. Look for a reward that will gratify even your soul. You can go for a spiritual experience and see life in a whole new way.

The core of your selection should be of self-compassion. Be kind to yourself, because of the benefits of self-kindness are numerous and overwhelming. It should not be a one-time reward but should be practiced as much as possible whenever a task is completed.

2. **It Infuses Positivity**

Your rewards should also drive you towards accomplishing more than you have achieved before. Acknowledge all of the things that you have achieved now but strive to do more in no time. Your reward should remind you about the importance of not being too hard on yourself.

3. There Should be a Necessary Balance in the Reward System

Don't allow your reward system to go over the top. There has to be a sensible balance. The reward should not exceed the size of the completed tasks that necessitated them.

4. Tone it Down

Sometimes your reward can come from within you, just something inside of you. It can just be a quiet day or moment when you sit and reflect everything on your journey. That can be a clear moment of enlightenment that will assist you in your future journey.

5. You don't have to spend a lot to reward yourself.

Rewards can simply be the things you enjoy doing.

6. It should be easy to achieve as fast as possible.

Here are some quick ways in which you can reward yourself after completing a task. There is a wide variety, and it is up to you to choose the one that suits you.

1. Go to a concert.
2. Visit a carnival or a music festival.
3. Go see a movie with some friends.
4. Listen to a captivation podcast.
5. Plan a night out with family members.
6. Enjoy a magazine read with a glass of cold juice.
7. Soak your body in a hot bath in the bathtub.
8. Stream some danceable music online.
9. Stream some interesting documentaries on Netflix.
10. Go for a long walk in your favorite park.
11. Join an exercise or dance class.
12. Visit an art gallery and see inspiring artwork.
13. Treat yourself to a foreign meal.

14. Visit a spa and get a royal treatment.
15. Have a picnic at a nearby beach.
16. Attend a sports event and cheer your favorite team.
17. Have a small get-together and celebrate with your friends.
18. Engage your hands in an art form that you love or in gardening.
19. Reorganize your room and closet.
20. Take photos of yourself.
21. Get a new hairdo.
22. Have a free day where you lie around, doing what you want or doing nothing at all. (But don't allow the pleasure of such a day get into your head. Once the day is over you go back to your routine.)
23. Write a short story about yourself and share it on social media.
24. Buy a new perfume with a fragrance that you love.
25. Get yourself some new clothes and discard off some old ones. Or you can give them out too.
26. Travel to a place you have always wanted to travel to.

CHAPTER SIX: NEW YOU, NEW ROUTINES

Growth in itself is the influence of greatness and achievement. Life has taught us to improve on everything, even the most common of things. Human beings are not separate from becoming better. We have come to learn the hard way through trial and error. And for this, history has related the importance of self-growth and the attitude needed to attain this level of excellence.

From the values required to the skills and knowledge needed, all these virtues can be learned. And the truth lies in the opportunity life has presented to learn continuously. The more we see the need to adopt new techniques and learn skills, the more comfortable living becomes. And since we don't live in isolation, the people around us get motivated through our process of learning. For example, renowned leaders invest a great time in knowledge and research; for that's one of the ways to break through to attainment.

Learning comes with many hurdles to climb, and no one says it's easy to adopt a new behavior. The fuel to sustain this change mostly comes from proven structures. One of them has to do with you. It is a positive attitude to see beyond your immediate mindset and embrace the newness you have seen people become. Once your mind is open, every other thing that relates to tranquility, togetherness, goal setting, and discipline will be natural to you. Your mind will now become fertile ground for breeding positive habits. You would be able to think brightly and expect the best to happen always.

A new routine begins with a firm conviction to do things differently. You might be tired of the results you make per time, and you feel something is missing. You are correct! If you have been thinking in this direction, then, you are ready to make an impact. This level is the foundation of your success. It is now evident that you are prepared to stand out without losing your uniqueness.

Don't be overwhelmed with the desire to get great results; it is attainable. But you need to understand that it is not automatic. The process involved needs you to review your choices creatively. You might also need to break down your preferences, emotions, and thought patterns to sooth the new routine you have chosen. Be sure that trends do not influence your choice to do things differently. Trends are like fashion; they come and vanish with time.

8 Ways to Create Great Habits that Lead to Success

The undeniable truth about success is that it has to be maintained. Sustaining excellence, achievement, and productivity starts with the most ignored principle. This standard is what I call the "principle of continuous growth." It deals with a conscious effort to regularly checkmate human composition to become better. Checkmating here means consistent appraisal of our emotions, skills, abilities, values, and attitudes to fit into the intended learning process. You need to ask questions to look for solutions instead of dwelling on the adverse reports.

How humans spend time goes a long way in accounting for productivity. The attitude put to the time also has a significant effect on whether the moment is valid or not. Certain elements might have acclimatized themselves to our views, making us prone to its negative impact. Such properties become our daily reference, disposition, belief, assumption, perception, and doctrine. Those are what result in habit, and we unconsciously repeat the pattern in our daily lives. The excellent news about a habit is that it can be learned. Your awareness of this routine and willingness to change is what matters most. I will outline below some great patterns that will inspire you to a successful life.

1. **Identify the Kind of Routine you Want.**

When a destination is known, the path to get there will be quite straightforward. See to it that you have convinced yourself of the kind of habit you want to break. This realization should be what matters most to you at the moment; a top priority that should not be postponed. Engage this decision in your thoughts consistently, but don't get carried away.

Identifying a negative habit is great; positioning your mind to replace it with a positive one will be more fulfilling. Satisfy your conscience and willpower to get set on the new journey of an improved person. It is necessary to be inwardly persuaded because that is the fuel that keeps the consistency going.

This stage of identification needs a proper breakdown of your engagement. Let's start with the little things that keep you busy like gossip. You need to know when and how the chat starts if your new routine is to get focused on writing a 1000-word report on safety per day every time you close from work. Then shut down any signal that suggests a delay in time and mental capabilities. While it might have been a frequent occurrence to chat at the parking lot, decide to shorten the discussion when you notice it's going south. You are in charge here, and that's the reason you need to be sincere. This is just an example, and yours might be different.

Also, realize that you will be in charge of your activities since you could predict what you desire. No one forced you into it; it's a personal choice so that mindfulness will set in. You would be able to position yourself to the present target and not get overwhelmed with the uncertainties of the future.

With the awareness of the present, you will be able to channel your energy and resources to achieving a present task. It will be more comfortable to accept the feelings and thoughts pattern that follows awareness.

Knowing what you want to achieve now and in the future places you on what it takes to attain them. Sacrifice is top of them. The newly identified routine is most likely not to follow your conventional way of life. And if yours is completely different, then get ready to adapt to the changes. Your time on the social network might need to change and hangout moments will adjust. Whatever it is you feel will be affected, prepare for it so as not to cause a delay along the path of successful attainment.

2. **Start From your Current Position.**

It might sound ridiculous when you see yourself not going at a fast pace. But the truth is, that is the perfect pace for you. Remember that habit constitutes a whole part of us, and the significant change won't come as quick as you imagine. The will to move is the necessary speed you need here.

Think of it as like building your muscles. You should know that the physical build-up won't surface in a day. You might be longing to stick to reading for three hours every evening. Understand that you would have used most of your productive moments during the day, and the possibility of reading at a stretch is slim since you are starting new. Why not start with thirty minutes and master the art for the first two weeks. Once you are consistent with the half an hour routine, increase the duration progressively. Ensure that you have established the behavior, and then seek to maintain it.

3. Recreate your Surroundings.

You are not the perfect composition of yourself without your environment. Some triggers stabilize your old habit, and most of them are within your reach. First, identify what they are and how they start. Those triggers might not signal delay and procrastination, but in the real sense, they are the villain.

Your new habit might be to start a new diet, but it seems your kitchen is still stuck with your old meals. It will be best to remove those foods or probably don't shop for them. It will be hard to focus on your new routine because the more you see those foods around, the harder it becomes to do away with them.

Reorganize your house, office, table, and even wardrobe to suit your expected behavior. The more you clear off distractions, the better your chance of success. The idea here is to get rid of the energy that makes learning difficult for you and replace it with good ones.

4. Move with People that Encourage you.

Your motivation for sticking to a learned behavior will be boosted when you are accountable to your friends. It is not compulsory to report to your acquaintance. It might be a colleague at work or your mentor. Choose someone you trust enough to criticize your report.

Your focus at this point is that you are not on the path of newness alone; there are external bodies that support your new habit. You will achieve optimum results if you choose someone successful in learning your selected routine. This way, he will be able to guide you constructively.

The significant result you want to see in the new routine can also be fostered when you see it as teamwork. Imagine your clique deciding to start a new habit. Every one of you will be motivated to put in your best. One good thing you will keep in mind is that "there is someone next to me I can always refer to," and he/she will be your most active encouragement. It will be difficult for you to stop. You might decide to speak your friends into learning a new behavior to enhance a fast rate of the result.

5. **Tell Others about your Plan.**

Most people are scared of failure, and failure in itself is an ailment that can be avoided. A better way humans prevent it is by pushing their energy to succeed. Think of yourself as someone that can be trusted with information. Confidentiality is not the highlight here but openness and accountability; knowing that a piece of you has been pre-committed to someone else. You will have to stick to your habit as a matter of necessity because you won't want to disappoint them.

You might start by informing some of your followers on social networks, friends, family members, and colleagues. Tell them beforehand and continuously engage them in your commitment routine. You might not want to disappoint them by backing off. Each time you face the temptation of going back, it's most likely to remember those you have pledged to.

6. **Work Out your New Habit in the Line of the Old.**

The energy involved in learning a new pattern is quite different from the complacent comfort of the old one. You will agree that the old routine would have gained access-control over you. Your life would have been repositioned to think and work in that direction. Telling you to dump the old habit immediately will be like asking you to change your skin color thrice a week. It is best to adjust your new behavior with the old one. Remember our first point to start small.

Since you have a plan already, make your strategy as flexible as possible. Be careful here as not to fall prey to negative thoughts. Your tendencies to flow with your daily experience will remind you of negativity, replace them with positive affirmations. As much as you commit to the new behavior steadily, you will get to become better and progress to become a different person.

7. **Reward Every Stage of Progress.**

Take note of your progress and commend every fulfillment of your desired results. No one can encourage you better than yourself. Reward here should not force you to remain on the spot. If you feel that you have not been motivated to do more while applauding yourself, change how you apply it. Create a conditional reward system. Watch the movie after you have finished off the report. Enjoy the evening with your clique whenever your room is perfectly clean. You can go with the flow of your reward after you have achieved your targets.

8. **Engage in Mental Exercise**

Your brain is not isolated from your new routine. Your cognitive capabilities have a significant role to play after your willpower. Start with your regular exercise, which might be walking around the park or jogging. While doing any of those exercises, think of the new habits you want to create. Allow your brain to process the information into consciousness, but don't get overwhelmed. This state of knowledge allows you to come into the present realities all the time. You will now be able to avoid distractions because your brain has processed your new routine into its system.

Remember that every makeup of your body matters, and your brain shouldn't be left out. You might also consider doing the exercises that sharpen focus given in this book.

9 Morning Routine to Make Every Day a Good Day

Nature has loaded a bountiful pack of benefits to the early hours of the day. And you will agree that creativity and innovation tend to flow freely during this time. Although this varies from the kind of person you are, it still does not negate how productivity can be achieved. This section will provide activities to perform to maximize your morning. Following them promptly will set the tone for an excellent day.

1. Make a Journal of your Thoughts and Use it for your Day.

The refreshing times of the morning are the best moment to write down what comes to your mind. Every one of your activities during the day might defer you the privilege, and that's why you must maximize the opportunity the early hours give.

Note that you might not need to do this brief exercise the conventional way. Be flexible enough to go with the flow of your thoughts. It might only involve ten minutes of your time. The bright side of journaling your opinion is that your brain is connected to a source of mindfulness. You won't need to stress your cognitive capability to remember the little things that flood your heart. Now you will be conscious of every idea that would boost your daily experience.

If you will need to create an outline of your thoughts, list them out! You may want to replicate writing the results of daily views. This action will make you reference your success story and remind you of your previous wins. You would also be able to repeat the same routine that brings achievement the next time you face a seemingly related challenge.

2. Fix your Bed

Does it sound a bit stressing? Yes! Because you have not been practicing it. This simple homemaking skill gives you a sense of responsibility for yourself. Your bed has been able to create the first task of the day successfully. Prove to yourself how successful you want this to be. Every time you do this excellently well, you build a sense of fulfillment.

3. Don't Conclude on Essential Decisions

Instinct might have guided you before now, but reality is not a game of chance; it will surely play out its rule. Leave your thoughts on the paper and get to finalize them later in the day. Most times, the inner will to make a perfect decision might not be strong enough to give an accurate strategy needed in achieving your goals. Be patient enough to research your perceived inspiration. Your search throughout the day will enhance better mental productivity for the subsequent mornings.

4. Limit your Choices

This early period of the day forces you to make the inevitable choice for your day. Streamline your selection to your set of values. You might be bugged with the color, type of shirt, shoe, and gown to wear. The accessories to use might even eat up a lot of your thinking time. Create a routine of your basic needs in the morning and make it practicable. For example, wake up, meditate, choose my clothing, bathe, make coffee, organize, and get set for the day. Simplify your daily choices, and don't make it grievous for yourself.

5. Energize your Body

Think of fitness as another tool to maintain a morning routine. You might not need to go jogging down the street. Your room can allow you to sweat out the energy required for the day. Remember the conditional method of reward you read under creating a habit that leads to success? Make it work for you here also.

Do 15 to 30 push-ups, after which you consider reviewing your activities for the day. You may also want to outstretch your arms and legs and then think about the day's task. Going through those exercises would have prepared your body for the job of the day. Your mind now will be at rest, and your happiness level is increased for the rest of the day.

6. Affirmations

Positive thinking, they say, result in a positive result. Create a mind full of positivity as you make affirmations that will reframe your mind. You often see through your mind; making it a necessity to flush out negativity for the day. Remember, it requires self-talk. Take out time to write your affirmations and read it to yourself. You may start with the simple challenge you had the day before and make good out of it. For example, say, "I walked with excellence today." "I achieved and surpassed targets today." "I am not overwhelmed with success or failure. I excel in my entire task."

7. Focus More on your Inner Self

The strength received from meditation can be enough to pull one through the mental challenges of the day. You will achieve this level of calmness when you separate yourself from both external and inward attachment. Create the willingness to break from the outer world for the moment. Breaking here means creating a focus on yourself, especially your willpower.

Note that this simple exercise requires you to clear off every thought and worry. Your anxiety level must be consciously reduced at this period. Look only at yourself, and not even at social networks. Plan to achieve this rare routine from your evening. No early checking of emails, Facebook, and blogs. Just you alone.

Disassociate yourself from your daily routine of dullness and inactiveness for this brief period in the morning. A 15-minute moment of reflection is a good start for you. See the possibility of attaining success for the day. Reflect on the affirmations you have made and see yourself achieving them. You are feeding your soul at this point to have a winning mindset. And that's how best to describe your day for anyone.

8. **Try a Cold Shower**

You might not be comfortable with this for the first time. But you can try it a few times and make a habit of it intermittently. Think of the advantages it comes with. Your blood flow tends to increase and makes you active for the day. You would be brave to start and doing this releases dopamine into your body. Your body is then left with the feeling of activeness, motivation, and pleasure. The bath will be an excellent icing to design the day.

9. **Plan for a Healthy Breakfast**

Understand the healthiness of feeding in the morning. It is essential to combine certain nutrients like protein, minerals, and vitamins together to have a great appetite and to fulfill nutritional needs. Although other nutrients are also necessary, healthy fats and proteins help stabilize your emotions. Remember that your mood needs to be right. Take, for example, a fiber-rich toast and topping. The fiber in this food helps slow digestion, enhancing stable blood sugar. Think of other simple but healthy meals for your breakfast.

6 Evening Routines to Ensure Tomorrow is just as Good as Today.

The best day results from a well-planned evening. Opportunities are loaded in the evening when you take up the challenge to be responsive. Understand what you need to do right before going to bed. Those activities will make up your evening routines. I know that your day might have made you weary, but you can readjust your mood and mental activeness. You can make your rest a blissful experience.

1. Reflect on your Day.

What happened at work today? Why was I issued a query letter? Ask many questions as possible. You deserve to know what has taken up your entire day. Use this period to identify the cause of your actions. Why did I react badly to a customer? Why was I angry during the lunch break? Don't stop with asking questions; break your query down to triggers. See what makes you do a particular thing.

Reflection doesn't mean you should use this period to think of your inadequacies alone. You might want to think of your targets that you met or surpassed. Do a proper assessment of your day's activities to know what goals to set for the other days.

2. Make a List of your Goals.

Look into the future of productivity and plan what you desire to attain. This process must be intentional because you might not have analyzed the challenges of the day. Design another structure to help you achieve more. Give a proper definition to your destination. Ensure that you eliminate rigidity in your approach to take in the future. After you have drafted out your goals, paste it where you could easily see it. It could be on your reading table or at the back of your door. Build an assurance that you are set for the following morning. Plan for your breakfast, your choice of clothes, and your time to wake up. It might take some time to get ready if you are doing it for the first time. Consistency in setting goals for the next day result in becoming an active organizer in the long run. Waking up to this reality helps you set your mind on attaining targets.

You may also want to read your goals to yourself. Just as you recite your affirmations, your attention in doing this is to activate mindfulness. Live in the reality of having your goals in your mind

3. Take Time to Read.

Engage your mind in learning something new! Doing this will get you ready for the following day. You might not need to do the long hours as you might be tired of the day's work. You might want to use this period to develop ideas you have written down in the morning. Research also on your challenge at work and learn from the experience of professionals.

4. Read up Affirmations.

Just like how you began your day with words of positivity, you might consider ending your day with it as well. Since you have reflected and analyzed the happenings of the day, use your conclusion to say beautiful things to your consciousness. You may say, "I was not overwhelmed because of failure." "I achieved better than I did today." "I see myself attaining my career goals." "My tomorrow is active and vibrant, and I stay happy with my friends and colleagues." Design your affirmations to suit your value.

5. Chat with your Family.

Bonding together as a family is an excellent ritual to practice. Take time out to say personal things to your spouse and children. And if you are single or living alone, find a means of communicating with your family. Every part of your discussion here should center on the family needs. Find out what your daughter desires of you. Inform her also of what you require of her to become successful in life. You might not want to do the job of a life coach every night, but ensure you build intimacy with your family. Also, engage your spouse in an intimate discussion. You may seek ideas relating to your work schedules and pattern.

6. Don't Give in to Idleness.

Setting yourself up for what to do does not mean doing anything, it means doing a specific task. Think of a job that will boost your mental alertness. Reading, meditation, exercise, cooking, etc. may be an excellent task to perform. Avoid the trap of getting caught up in a massive job for the evening. The blue screen should be a thing to avoid at this time.

Since you need to start small, you may also think of fixing your clutter. Arrange the pile of books on the table and clear your wardrobe.

CHAPTER SEVEN: NO MORE OBSTACLES

7 Ways to Conquer Your Fear of Failure

It is natural to fear. It is one of the things that make us human. Fear will always present itself whenever you are about to embark on a brand-new venture. Yet fear, too, can be very dangerous. It can hold you back from accomplishing what you need to accomplish.

Fear can manifest itself in a lot of ways. There is the fear of heights, the fear of rising water, and the fear of spiders, and so on. But as regards being productive, the fear that relates to us the most is the fear of failure.

Failure is absolutely nothing to be afraid of. Even the richest, the most powerful, and the most successful amongst us have once experienced failure at one point in time or another. So, if you ever fail, you should know that you are not alone. You will get through it.

It is just like falling sick. People put in a lot of measures in place so that they don't fall sick. Unfortunately, no matter how much they try, they ultimately fall sick one day. What do you do in that situation? You don't run away from sickness; you fight it. And once it leaves you, your body learns and adapts so that the next time there is an attack from that pathogen, it will know how to react and protect you.

The same goes for your failure. Learn from it. Build your stamina from it. When it first hits you, it will seem like your world is about to crumble to pieces, but I assure you that it will only be for a moment. These tips will help you manage and overcome the fear of failure:

1. **Stand Up to it.**

Life is a battleground. If you are not ready to fight, then get ready to live a miserable life. Nothing will ever be handed over to you on a platter of gold, except if your family has stacks of gold bars somewhere in the World Bank. To see success, to have accomplishments, you should know that you will have to stand up to your fear of failure. The fear of failure is not failure itself, but it is a strong pathway that leads towards failure. The best you can do for yourself is to push yourself out of that pathway into the pathway of success.

2. **Show yourself some Kindness.**

Don't beat yourself down. Don't be too harsh on yourself. Understand that the fear you have for failure is something natural; but it doesn't mean that you are not good enough. Nobody is good enough; we are all striving to be better. So, don't beat yourself up simply because you did not hit the mark the first time. There are still a lot of open opportunities for you to try and be better.

3. **Understand that Failing Once does not Make you a Complete Failure.**

You only become a total failure when you decide to give and stop chasing. The point where you decide to give up becomes the point where your success story ends, so it all depends on you and how well you choose to maximize your strengths. A lot of successful figures that we look up to today once failed, but that didn't make them consider themselves failures. They kept up with the struggle and brought something admirable.

4. **Feed your Mind with Optimism.**

A lot of people experience failure every day, but that doesn't mean that you must be one of them. A thought will present itself and ask you, "What if you fail?" I want you to challenge that thought by asking, "What if I succeed?" People fail, and people also succeed. It all depends on the group you decide to identify yourself with. If there is ever going to be a successful person in that field, then it could be you.

5. **Free yourself from the Obsession of Perfectionism**

Many people have been tied down because of the need to get it right the first time. You don't have to get it right the first time. Have that at the back of your mind. Nothing good that was ever created was perfect in one go. Accept the fact that you might not hit your target at first, but that does not mean that you will stop trying. The process of trying to perfect something is itself a learning process. As you keep on doing that, you will keep getting better at it until you become as good as you want to be.

6. **Why do you Fear Failure?**

For some people, the fear of failure stems from all the things they have heard about failure. Others just don't want others to see them as a failure. Hence, they begin to nurture fear for it. Whatever the case may be, try to find out the reason why you fear failure and do well to tackle it early. Are you afraid because you do not fully understand the task at hand? Then do well to understand it better. Are you afraid because you have heard scary stories of people who encountered failure? Then begin to put things in place that will help you overcome failure.

7. **Accept failure for what it is**

Failure is not a monster, nor is it a beast. It can only become as large as tormenting as you want it to be at any point in time. You define what your failure becomes for you. Seeing failure as something that will come and go, something that will come and pass, a fleeting moment in our lives, will help you to overcome your fear for it easily.

7 Strategies for Defeating the Monster of Perfectionism

To be perfect is an admirable quality, and a lot of people will die for that quality, to be free of any form of stain or blemish. Seeking to attain perfection will drive you towards producing work of high standards. To strive for perfection is not wrong in any way; in fact, it is quite necessary to produce work that will stand the test of time.

However, the pursuit of perfection can easily become an obsessive behavior if it is not left unchecked. People who pursue this are referred to as perfectionists, and most of the time, their standards are hardly ever met. This can, in turn, lead to a sort of frustration.

These perfectionists are never happy with anything until it meets their insanely high standards. Conversely, perfectionists seem always to want to put off some tasks simply because they are scared that they will never carry out that task well enough. This can somehow become a killer of productivity because such a person will never want to break into any new adventure and see what happens with it.

A piece of advice I always give to people is that they should learn to work with their perfectionism. Don't allow your high standards to hold you back from performing; instead make it work for you to produce a more admirable job. You do that by starting up the task. Drop your fear of imperfection and just start. Complete the task; and after completion, you can go back and add your touch of perfectionism to it.

The life of a perfectionist is quite boring because nothing new is ever explored. That shouldn't be the case with you. That is why you will need to get over your perfectionist mindset but not your high standards. Understand that perfection can never be attained, ever. Instead, you can keep getting better and better. Here are some strategies you can employ to help you overcome perfectionism:

1. **Learn to Accept When it is Good Enough When you have Put in your Whole Best.**

Like I clearly stated, perfection is a myth. Even when you think you have achieved it, if you look closer, you will see that there are still flaws. You can literally drive yourself crazy. Try to understand when you have done enough in a particular project. Good is never enough, but your best can always suffice. Don't stress your mind. The best thing to do is to get into the flow and allow yourself to be moved ahead with it. You don't have to produce perfect work; all you have to do is produce your best work.

2. **Understand that Perfectionism is a Time Killer**

There are two major problems I have with perfectionists: the first is that they hardly ever start any task for fear of not producing to their standards. The second is that even when they begin a task, they spend a lot of time going through the steps, repeating them, just to produce a perfect job. The amount of time wasted is even enough to get them to ignore the job and get frustrated. No one is saying that you should not take your time. What I am saying is do not kill your time. These are two different concepts, and they mean different things. Take your time and give your the best. Know when to stop and leave the rest. There is only enough you can give to any project.

3. **Understand that you can Hurt People with your Perfectionist Standards.**

As has been pointed out before, never lower your standards, aim for the best quality, but not necessarily perfection. Perfection is unattainable. One thing about striving for perfection and high standards is that you are capable of hurting the people around you with your standards. Not everyone is like you. Not everyone is a perfectionist like you. Some people only want to put in their best into what they do, and that is all. When you continue to drop the weight of your unachievable standards on them, you can crush them and make them hate you. Nothing they will ever do will ever be enough for you, and this alone is capable of hurting your relationship with them. Make sure to get the best from your employees and workers at all times, but don't become a frustrating master that can never be pleased.

4. **Eliminate the Competitive Mindset.**

For a lot of perfectionists, their character stems from being the best at all times. They want no other person ever to be ahead of them, and it frustrates them when their plans don't go as intended. There is a kind of competition known as the healthy competition, and that is the kind of competition that you should strive towards. Subscribe to the competition that brings out the best in you instead of dragging you towards envy.

Another thing you should understand is that you are your own biggest competitor. All you have to do is develop on yesterday, build on the success you have had in the past. And come to think of it, if you were perfect yesterday, what do you want to do today. Life is an adventure, and perfectionism breaks that adventure. It hinders you from discovering treasures. So, stay free and keep your mind on your own self.

5. **Eliminate Perfectionism Triggers in your Life.**

This will involve looking into a lot of things. Sometimes the people in your life may also be some of the factors causing your obsession with perfectionism. Because they are perfectionists themselves, they will do everything in their power to seek the same from you. Don't buy into that. Perfectionism, as I have explained to you, is stressful. It is left for you to carry out an inner analysis and identify all those things that trigger perfectionism in your life. Quench them.

6. **Reevaluate your Standards**

Perfectionism is a result of excessively high standards. You need to check yourself so you don't wreck yourself. It is not normal to expect a 3-year-old to be able to spell five-letter words correctly without missing out on any letters. But a perfectionist doesn't care. They just want it to be done, and they will have no idea that they are hurting that child.

Ask yourself if your standards are unrealistically high. Once you identify the high standards, you can then tone them down so that everybody benefits from it. You can also ask people around you who will be willing to help you identify those standards that you have to work on.

7. **Allow Imperfection Sometimes.**

You don't always have to perfect. We live in an imperfect world, yet we all enjoy the world and don't want to leave. The truth is that you can do with some imperfection in your life. Leave the bedsheets rough and rumpled as you leave the house. Allow the kids to dress themselves up. Just challenge any perfectionist tendencies you may have and see what happens.

7 Ways in Which Positivity can Manifest Success

Positivity, as a trait, does not mean smiling all the time and always carrying a cheerful look. It is way more profound than that. Positivity really has to do with your overall perspective of life. It is all about what you make with whatever life gives you at the moment, either negative or positive. "When life throws lemons at you, you make lemonade" is one quote that adequately captures the essence of positivity.

Research has proven over time that people who are happier, people who have more positivity in their lives, generally end up more successful than those who do not buy into the message of positivity. Positivity has been linked to better performance and productivity in workplaces. The presence of positive emotions always makes the generation of wonderful ideas. Some major benefits of positivity include:

- **Better mental performance and sharper response to stimuli.** Positive people generally tend to have brains that perform better and produce better results. Their mind travels wider during a brainstorm session, and they can come up with a wide range of ideas for a project. Ultimately, this leads to being more creative and productive people.
- **People tend to get closer to those who already carry a lot of positivity in them.** Positivity in a relationship also helps to build a strong and lasting connection between the parties involved.
- **The health benefits associated with positivity are enormous.** In fact, positivity can cause a person to eat healthier because their minds are always sharp to point out the things they should not be taking into their system. Depression, which is a by-product of negative thinking, has been connected to overweight and junk feeding. A positive mindset will mean a lower heart rate, lower blood pressure, and lower stress. People who stay positive are also known to sleep better.
- **Positivity helps to build a psychology of confidence, boosted self-esteem, and bodily energy.** With such energy to expend, positive people achieve their goals quite faster than non-positive people.

With all of these benefits listed, you can now see that it is quite important that you develop a positive mindset that will fuel your success. The question now is how you can do that. These strategies will help you:

1. **Keep your Focus on all the Good Things in your Life.**

Nobody has it all beautiful for them. We all have our ups and downs, where we face a lot of challenges daily. But the question remains how do you allow those challenges to define you? Of course, you will face the door, but you will also face up. How well do you keep your gaze on the good things in your life? Remember that every single day comes with its own benefits, no matter how bad that day goes. Learn to focus on these benefits for as long as you can.

2. **Learn all the Lessons that Life Throws at you.**

As I have stated numerous times in this book, every failure you come across in your life is a lesson if only you will choose to learn from it. Failures are prone to breed negative thoughts in your mind. These include: "I am not good enough." "I will never be worth it." and "I won't make it." But remember that each time you stumble in the dark, your body learns of obstacles on that path and never makes the same mistake again. That is why you can walk into your room even with the light off and make your way to the switch without hitting your toes on the cabinet.

3. **Encourage Yourself.**

No one can talk to you like you can talk to yourself. There is no better motivation than the one you give yourself. Wake up each morning, look at yourself in the mirror, and release transformative mantras into your day. There is something about the words we speak. They possess a very strong creative power that can go ahead and provide us with the best results. Some people use this power to produce very negative results for themselves because they are always talking about the bad in their lives. These thoughts have a way of building strongholds in your mind and control you. Never allow them to do that. Always be the one in control and dictate what comes into your life.

4. **Keep your Mind on the Things Happening in your Present.**
The present is your now, your reality at this moment, the things that are currently happening in your life. Some people live their lives for the future, while others live in the past. But I tell you that the most important time to live for is now. Don't lose your existence while chasing other realities.

5. **Keep Positive People and Positivity Around you.**
A wall of negative thoughts is always on the rise in our mind, and it totally depends on you to determine if it continues to rise or it crumbles to the ground. You can destroy any form of negative walls by surrounding yourself with positive people and positive things. All of these will assist you in choking down any negativity bridling up around you. Find most people and place them around your life. Talk to them as much as you can and try to learn from them. They have a way of affecting yours into positivity.

6. **Focus on your Goals.**

Negative thoughts are a form of distraction that results because people aren't obsessed with reaching their goals. A mind that stays focused on achieving goals and being the best will never have time to nurture any form of negativity. Keep yourself productive at all times, and continue to focus on how you can achieve more and outdo yourself.

7. **Practice Gratefulness.**

This is one of the greatest tools you can use to activate a positive mindset for success. When you continue to stay grateful and thankful for the things around you, you rarely have time to think about the negatives.

5 Empowering Mantras to Destroy Self-Sabotage and Start Getting Stuff Done.

Funny enough, there has always been this kind of mythological attachments to the word "mantra." It has suffered almost the same fate as "meditation," where someone thinks it can only apply to a Buddhist monk in Tibet or a witch sitting on the Himalayas. Most times, we don't even understand how powerful mantras are and how they can help us generally.

What exactly is a mantra if you should use it? Take it this way: a mantra is a mind tool or a word, sentence, or sound that is used to keep your mind in place and prevent it from wandering off into distraction. Mantras can help you out in different facets of our life if they are employed in the right way. They can help you become more productive. They can help you to stay focused. They can help you to reframe your mind and the thoughts that swirl in it. The possibilities are endless, and that is why it is necessary that you begin to employ mantras in these different facets of your life so that you have the best of it. Here are some mantras that can help you overcome yourself and start getting stuff done.

1. **I accept peace into my life and my daily activities**.

You can assist this mantra to come to fulfillment by visualizing that peace that you desire over and over until it manifests itself. You can make use of this mantra to call peace into any aspect of your life: your mind, your soul, your work etc. When these words are repeated over time, your mind begins to believe them and align towards having them accomplished.

2. **I will strive for the best instead of striving for perfection**.

We have gone through this, and I have explained how toxic perfectionism can be to you and the people around you. Make use of this mantra to overcome a mindset of perfectionism. Before you start an important task, you can repeat it over and over until your mind assimilates it. When you find yourself gradually falling into that mindset of perfectionism, repeat it, and give yourself the required focus.

3. My mistakes are for my benefits.

Playing the blame game is always easy, and this mantra is here to help you do the exact opposite of that. Use this mantra when you have made a stupid mistake and feel like you are a failure. Keep it from time to time, even as your mind may try to make you feel bad about the decisions you may have made in the past.

4. I will focus on my present.

The mantra is most importantly used when you noticed your mind gradually slipping back to your past or worrying about the future. Remind yourself using this mantra to keep your focus on the present.

5. I will meet my deadlines and achieve all my goals.

Use this mantra at the beginning of each day, first thing after you wake in the morning or while washing your mouth. As you repeat this mantra to yourself, continue to visualize what you accomplished goals will look like. Ruminate over all the exciting benefits open to you as you hit your daily targets.

CONCLUSION

I want to appreciate you for following me on this journey, for preserving and being here until this moment. In fact, thank you for not procrastinating the reading of this book. I believe you have skipped pages but read through the book with all diligence.

Throughout this book, I have done everything possible to help you understand the concept of procrastination and how it works. We have explored some of the major triggers of procrastination and also the main ways in which you can get over and conquer these triggers. But I can tell you that regardless of the wealth of knowledge hidden in this book, this is not all it takes.

I can tell you that we all face our own different procrastination triggers that are specific to each and every one of us. While reading a book, I am quite certain that you encounter the one that most related to your situation. These are the issues that you need to address as soon as possible. You cannot change everything at once. Try and employ some strategy to your action plan in defeating procrastination.

It is one thing to own the rod, and it is another thing to strike the snake. Most people will go to any length to acquire the rod but will never take action to strike the snake until it bites. I want to tell you that you can break free from the grip of procrastination today, if only you will decide to take action and follow the instructions listed in this book. There will be a point where you will feel like you have failed when it will seem like you should just give up and stop trying, but don't allow that stop you. Promise yourself that you will fight right till the end. Only keep your focus on making some small necessary changes and see your life improve every day.

www.ingramcontent.com/pod-product-compliance
Lightning Source LLC
Chambersburg PA
CBHW022013120526
44592CB00034B/805